Enduring Faith

An 8-Week Devotional Study
of the Book of Hebrews

by Nivine Richie

ENDURING FAITH: AN 8-WEEK DEVOTIONAL STUDY OF THE BOOK OF HEBREWS
Published by Lighthouse Publishing of the Carolinas
2333 Barton Oaks Dr., Raleigh, NC, 27614

ISBN 978-1-941103-11-1
Copyright © 2014 by Nivine Richie
Cover design by writelydesigned.com
Interior design by Karthick Srinivasan

Available in print from your local bookstore, online, or from the publisher at: www.lighthousepublishingofthecarolinas.com

For more information on this book and the author visit: www.unfoldinghisword.com

All rights reserved. Non-commercial interests may reproduce portions of this book without the express written permission of Lighthouse Publishing of the Carolinas, provided the text does not exceed 500 words.

When reproducing text from this book, include the following credit line: "Enduring Faith: An 8-Week Devotional Study of the Book of Hebrews by Nivine Richie published by Lighthouse Publishing of the Carolinas. Used by permission."

Commercial interests: No part of this publication may be reproduced in any form, stored in a retrieval system, or transmitted in any form by any means—electronic, photocopy, recording, or otherwise—without prior written permission of the publisher, except as provided by the United States of America copyright law.

All Scripture quotations, unless otherwise indicated, are taken from The Holy Bible, English Standard Version. Copyright ©2000; 2001 by Crossway Bibles, a division of Good News Publishers. Used by permission. All rights reserved.

Scriptures marked "AMP" are taken from The Amplified Bible, New Testament. Copyright© 1954, 1958, 1987, by The Lockman Foundation. Used by permission.

Scriptures marked "NIV" are taken from the Holy Bible, New International Version®. NIV®. Copyright© 1973, 1978, 1984 by International Bible Society. Used by permission of Zondervan. All rights reserved.

Scriptures marked "NKJV" are taken from the New King James Version. Copyright© 1982 by Thomas Nelson, Inc. Used by permission. All rights reserved.

Scriptures marked "KJV" are taken from the King James Version of the Bible. Public Domain.

Lyrics of "In Christ Alone," written by Keith Getty and Stuart Townend. Copyright©2002 Thankyou Music (PRS) (adm. Worldwide at CapitolCMGPublishing.com excluding Europe which is adm. By Kingswaysongs) All rights reserved. Used by permission of Capitol CMG Publishing. License no. 545682.

Brought to you by the creative team at LighthousePublishingoftheCarolinas.com: Denise Loock

Library of Congress Cataloging-in-Publication Data

Richie, Nivine

Enduring Faith: An 8-Week Devotional Study of the Book of Hebrews/Nivine Richie/1st ed.

Printed in the United States of America

Dedication

For Pat

Table Of Contents

Preface 1
Getting the Most Out of This Study 4

Week 1: Jesus, The Reliable Object of Our Faith 6
   Day 1. Jesus, The Word of God 8
   Day 2. Jesus, Higher Than the Angels 11
   Day 3. Jesus, the Alpha and Omega 14
   Day 4. Jesus, Our Salvation 17
   Day 5. Jesus Succeeded Where Adam Failed 20

Week 2: Jesus Invites Us To Cease from Our Works and Enter His Rest 24
   Day 1. Our Kinsman Redeemer 26
   Day 2. The House That Christ Built 29
   Day 3. A Time of Testing 33
   Day 4. Sin's Deceitfulness 36
   Day 5. Sabbath Rest 39

Week 3: Jesus Grants Us Access to the Throne of Grace 43
   Day 1. The Living, Active Word of God 45
   Day 2. Jesus, Our Great High Priest 49
   Day 3. Milk or Meat? 52
   Day 4. The Good Soil 55
   Day 5. Behind the Curtain 58

Week 4: Jesus, Our High Priest, Is Able To Completely Save Us 62
   Day 1. The Pre-Priesthood Priest 64
   Day 2. The Weak Levitical Priesthood 67
   Day 3. Holy, Blameless, Pure 71
   Day 4. A Shadow of What Is in Heaven 74
   Day 5. The New Covenant 77

Week 5: Jesus, the Superior and Final Sacrifice 81
    Day 1. The First Tabernacle 83
    Day 2. Without the Shedding of Blood 86
    Day 3. Once for All 90
    Day 4. The Superior Sacrifice 94
    Day 5. Made Perfect 97

Week 6: Jesus Credits Faith As Righteousness 101
    Day 1. Therefore, Let Us… 103
    Day 2. The Call To Persevere 106
    Day 3. By Faith We Understand 110
    Day 4. Commended by God 113
    Day 5. By Faith Abraham 116

Week 7: Faith Is Followed by Inheritance 120
    Day 1. By Faith Moses 121
    Day 2. Divine Approval 124
    Day 3. Those Things That Hinder 127
    Day 4. The Encouragement of Discipline 130
    Day 5. Citizens in Heaven 133

Week 8: Jesus Equips Us To Do His Will 137
    Day 1. The Kingdom That Cannot Be Shaken 139
    Day 2. Love Others 142
    Day 3. Legalism: A Strange Teaching 146
    Day 4. Outside the Camp 151
    Day 5. Final Exhortations 154

Endnotes 159
Acknowledgments 162

Praise for *Enduring Faith*

Concise, vital, rubber-meets-the-road Christian instruction. Plumbed from the riches of the book of Hebrews, *Enduring Faith* holds out a hand to the person who seeks greater faith and says, "Walk with Jesus—He's ALL you really need."

To a "no faith" generation, God has sent Nivine Richie to share her heart and hope. This study is destined to be a spiritual strength builder. I saw much more than an eight-week study . . . I saw Jesus!

~**Paul Waters**
Senior Pastor, Myrtle Grove Baptist Church
Wilmington, NC

Nivine Richie is a woman who knows God and understands His Word. She possesses a unique ability to lead believers into a deeper fellowship with Jesus Christ by conveying the truths of Scripture in a relevant, life-changing way. In an engaging and easy-to-follow path, Nivine helps us to navigate the waters of Hebrews so that we will "go on to maturity" (6:1) and receive a "great reward" (10:35).

~**Douglas H. Lyon, D.Min.**
Senior Pastor, Shiloh Bible Church
Bloomsburg, PA

The book of Hebrews is a powerful presentation of the excellency of Jesus Christ. Dr. Richie's study presents the leading ideas of Hebrews in an attractive form for people who seek to know what Christianity is all about.

Each study ends with pertinent questions that lead the student to think about God's Word. Although this study is primarily useful for personal and group Bible studies, preachers and other scholars should also get this book. I have not seen a better outline of Hebrews than the one Richie gives at the beginning. Great topics for expository teaching.

~**John F. Thornbury, Th.M., D.Min.**
Author of *God Sent Revival, System of Bible Doctrine,* and *David Brainerd*
Lexington, KY

So many Christians are not enjoying the abundant life Jesus promised them. Something is missing; it has been forgotten or neglected. Christians know what they should be, but they are not enjoying the fullness of what Jesus promised them.

In *Enduring Faith,* Nivine Richie reminds us that Jesus is the one object of our faith. He is sufficient. His work is complete in our behalf. Our problem is that we get our eyes off the Lord Jesus Christ and look at our circumstances and ourselves.

Hebrews is a difficult book for many, but *Enduring Faith* will help you transfer your faith from what you can do for Jesus to what He has done for you. The end result will be a life that is fruitful and contented in Jesus. I highly recommend *Enduring Faith*. It will help you learn to walk with your eyes fixed on Jesus, the Author and Finisher of our faith.

~**E. Truman Herring**
Author of *Spiritual Barrenness That Leads to Spiritual Fruitfulness*
Senior Pastor, Boca Glades Baptist Church
Boca Raton, FL

With great enthusiasm, I endorse this eight-week devotional study by Dr. Nivine Richie. Her balance of thoughtful commentary and her transparent personal illustrations drew me into God's presence and strengthened my faith.

This study will point you to Jesus Christ as the author and perfecter of your faith. Anyone who daily spends fifteen minutes on this study for eight weeks has made a wise investment that will pay off with an enduring faith.

~**Shane Hartley**
Senior Staff with Campus Crusade for Christ International
Wilmington, NC

What a gift! With its soul-searching insights and relatable word pictures, *Enduring Faith* brings the book of Hebrews to life. In a generation blown about by every wind of doctrine, this study could not be more timely. My heart's tether to Jesus Christ—the Anchor—is tightened for a faith that holds!

~**Mary Jane Waters**
Music Minister, Myrtle Grove Baptist Church,
Wilmington, NC

Nivine Richie is a great storyteller. She possesses the admirable gift of taking complicated biblical concepts and making them simple and understandable. This light and refreshing read will be a blessing and challenge to anyone!

~Sharon Gill
Founder and Chairman, Oasis Compassion Agency
Greenacres, FL

Nivine Richie tells stories and pertinent truth in a delightful manner. I loved *Enduring Faith* and was challenged more than once in my faith's endurance. I'm convinced this insightful study on honest faith will help readers explore their faith more deeply, and yet learn how to live it more practically.

~Robin Bryce
Ministry Entrepreneur, Minister's Wife, and Speaker/Author
Houston, TX

Enduring Faith is an enriching study on the book of Hebrews. I found it easy to understand with great, thought-provoking questions. The material is applicable to our daily lives.

~Judy Englund
Past Bible Study Director at New Braunfels Bible Church
New Braunfels, TX

Preface

Assault with intent to dismember. Christianity under attack. Unsure of what to believe, Americans are choosing to believe in nothing at all. A disturbing number of teenagers abandon the faith of their parents. Seven out of ten young people quit church by the time they are twenty-three. And though some return to church, many don't return by the age of thirty.[1] Sadly, the slice of the American population with no religious affiliation is our largest growing segment.[2]

Books, television, movies—many claim that our faith is groundless and demonstrates weakness, intellectual dullness. High school history books undermine Christianity, suggesting it is a religion cobbled together from other religions. Science books teach that man simply arrived on the planet by chance, without purpose and without hope.

How many times have we heard the following subtle, or not so subtle, lies? Follow your heart. Trust your gut. Believe in yourself. Biblical truth is discarded; philosophies that worship man are embraced. People gladly exchange the truth of God for a lie, but the devastating result is decay, foolishness, and hopelessness (Roman 1:25).

This short study is about faith—faith built on a sure foundation. That foundation is Christ alone: the superiority of Christ, the superiority of His work, and the superior lives we can lead when we build on that foundation. We don't need blind faith. Neither do we need to grit our teeth and block our ears to safeguard our faith. Yes, we want childlike faith, but that's not sightless faith.

God calls us to develop a faith that endures, and when circumstances seem to line up in our favor, we can be lulled into believing our faith is sturdy and indestructible. But is its foundation as solid as it should be? Are we relying on Jesus, or are we relying on our ability to believe in Jesus? We can have peace knowing that He is hanging on to us, not because we think we're hanging on to Him. Oswald Chambers said, "Faith that is sure of itself is not faith; faith that is sure of God is the only faith there is."[3] In other words, our faith is in Him, not in our faith.

One of the most powerful modern hymns, "In Christ Alone," is a reminder that our faith must be firmly anchored:

> In Christ alone my hope is found;
> He is my light, my strength, my song;
> This cornerstone, this solid ground,
> Firm through the fiercest drought and storm.
> What heights of love, what depths of peace,
> When fears are stilled, when strivings cease!
> My comforter, my all in all—
> Here in the love of Christ I stand.[4]

Jesus is both the *author* and the *finisher* of our faith (see Hebrews 12:2 NKJV, emphasis mine). He initiates and He completes. Not me. The basis of my peace, my faith, is knowing that He will hang on to me in spite of my weaknesses, in spite of my inability to hang on to Him. Over the next eight weeks, your faith will be strengthened as you study that Christ is who He claims to be; therefore, He is the only one who could do what He did so that we can live by faith in Him and cultivate a faith that endures.

As you start this study, my prayer for you is Ephesians 1:15-19:

> For this reason, because I have heard of your faith in the Lord Jesus and your love toward all the saints, I do not cease to give thanks for you, remembering you in my prayers, that the God of our Lord Jesus Christ, the Father of glory, may give you the Spirit of wisdom and of revelation in the knowledge of him, having the eyes of your hearts enlightened, that you may know what is the hope to which he has called you, what are the riches of his glorious inheritance in the saints, and what is the immeasurable greatness of his power toward us who believe.

No eloquent or lofty words can energize your faith. Only God can. Pray that He will give you the "Spirit of wisdom and revelation in the knowledge of him." May you know the hope, riches, and power that are yours when you live by faith in Christ alone. Amen.

Getting the Most Out of This Study

You don't have to be a theologian to study the Bible or to facilitate a Bible study. Your Bible and some time alone with God each day are all you need. This book is designed for self-study or for small group study. To get the most out of this Bible study, set aside about fifteen minutes each day to read the devotion, look up the related verses, answer the questions, and then spend a little time in reflection as you respond in the journal. That's it. Nothing fancy.

If you feel like you're too busy to commit to an eight-week Bible study, then this book is for you. The devotions are intentionally short, and yet they encourage you to look deeply into God's Word. Think of all the different ways we spend our fifteen-minute blocks of time each day. Many are filled with unavoidable activities, but I imagine if you examine your schedule, several blocks of time can be carved out and set aside for your spiritual health. Maybe the time spent waiting to pick up the kids at school or a few minutes alone in the car after lunch. A small investment of time can yield a great spiritual return. I know from personal experience that if you ask God to find time in your schedule, He will do it.

For Leaders

This study is most effective if you meet once a week to discuss the five devotions for that week. Encourage your group to do their "homework" so they are prepared for the discussion. Though some teachers insist that only those who have done their homework can participate in the discussion, I've found that restriction is unnecessary. A typical weekly meeting can be structured like this:

- Open with prayer.
- Select the main discussion questions from each devotion and ask volunteers to read the related passages aloud.
- If the group is large (over fifteen participants) or if the group is shy and quiet, encourage discussion by giving the members time to discuss their answers in small groups of two or three.

- Bring the full group back together and ask for volunteers to share their insights with the large group.

Over the years, I've collected some ideas that have worked for me as I lead large and small women's Bible study groups. I've learned to wait in silence after I ask a question, rather than jump in and answer the question myself. I've learned to rephrase the question if the original language didn't seem to draw any response from the class. These ideas and more are available to you at www.unfoldinghisword.com. Please check back as this teaching blog is updated regularly.

Any time invested in prayer and Bible study is time well spent. Abraham "grew strong in his faith as he gave glory to God, fully convinced that God was able to do what he had promised" (Romans 4:20-21). Bible study is convincing. We too can grow stronger in our faith when we are convinced that God is able to do what He has promised.

Week 1.
Jesus, The Reliable Object of Our Faith

Faith must have an object. Believing in something that's not reliable, or worse, something that doesn't exist is nothing more than a delusion. Recently, a wonderful teacher, Dr. John Lennox, said this:[5]

> Believing in the tooth fairy is a delusion. Why? Because the tooth fairy is not real. If God is not real, then Christianity is a delusion. But what if God is real? Then it is the atheists that are deluded.

Our faith is evidence-based faith. It is not blind faith nor is it wishful thinking. "But God demonstrates his own love for us in this: While we were still sinners, Christ died for us" (Romans 5:8 NIV). In the Greek, "demonstrates" is *sunestemi,* which means, "to set together, i.e. to introduce, or to exhibit."[6] *Vine's Expository Dictionary* adds, "To set one person or thing with another by way of presenting and commending." In other words, God shows us His love by using a contrast: by presenting Christ's perfection next to our sinfulness, we see just how much God loves us.

Throughout history, God has repeatedly confirmed His existence and His reliability. The things we read about in the New Testament—the blind seeing, the lame walking, the dead coming back to life—those events happened to real people and were witnessed by real people. They aren't myths. They are accounts and testimonies. In John's gospel we read, "Jesus did many other miraculous signs in the presence of his disciples, which are not recorded in this book. But these are written that you may believe that Jesus is the Christ, the Son of God, and that by believing you may have life in his name" (John 20:30-31 NIV).

The book of Hebrews begins by detailing Jesus' supremacy over all creation. The author lays out the case for Jesus being superior to the prophets and the angels. He existed before the world was formed, and He will continue to exist long after He brings this chapter of history to an end. He created us and He saved us. He is seated at the right hand of the Majesty on High where He continues to intercede for us today. Jesus is the object of our faith and He is reliable.

Day 1. Jesus, The Word of God

Long ago, at many times and in many ways, God spoke to our fathers by the prophets, but in these last days he has spoken to us by his Son, whom he appointed the heir of all things, through whom also he created the world.

Hebrews 1:1-2

In the first grade, our son brought home an assignment to write two sentences. One sentence had to be a question and the other a command. He showed us his homework when he finished: "Yasmeen, do you want to clean your room?"

"That's a good start, Joey," we said. "But where is your second sentence?"

He insisted that he only needed to turn in one sentence. "When mommy asks Yasmeen if she wants to clean her room, she's really telling her to clean her room." He understood the message—one sentence was both a question and a command.

Our God is creative. Throughout history, He spoke to His people in many ways, some of which have never been repeated. He spoke through prophets, dreams, a burning bush, angels, and a gentle whisper. He even spoke through a donkey! When God wants to be heard, He conveys His message in the manner He chooses, and at just the right time.

The opening verses of Hebrews tell us, "In these last days, he has spoken to us by his Son…" Communicating through a person? Yes, Jesus is *the* message; there is no other. The message is this: God loves people but He hates sin. He delivered it clearly in the person of Jesus Christ. God's message to humanity is fully wrapped up in Christ. In sending His Son to earth to die for our sins, God communicated His love for mankind and His judgment on sin. It's always been the same message—even when He spoke it through the prophets.

Read Today's Scripture:
Hebrews 1:1-4, John 1:1-8, Revelation 19:11-13

1. What name does Revelation 19:13 give the rider of the horse? Why is that significant?

   _____

   _____

   _____

   _____

2. Based on Hebrews 1:1–4 and John 1:1–8, how do you describe the Word of God?

   _____

   _____

   _____

   _____

3. Which of the Father's attributes have you learned to appreciate by understanding Jesus the Son?

   _____

   _____

   _____

   _____

10 | Enduring Faith

Today's Journal:
How did God deliver His message of salvation to you? Has He revealed any areas of your life where you need to strengthen your faith?

Through my sweet mother in law, who shared with me what it means to be saved and was patient and gentle in explaining what it means and takes to be saved.

Day 2. Jesus, Higher Than the Angels

For to which of the angels did God ever say, "You are my Son, today I have begotten you"?

Hebrews 1:5

Almost any school-aged child can tell you about a trick that students pull on teachers to redirect a class discussion. The teacher comes to class prepared to teach, but then one pupil asks an unexpected question, maybe slightly related to the topic at hand, maybe not. The teacher gladly answers the question, which leads to further discussion. Without warning, the actual topic for the day has been hijacked, and the students have successfully redirected the teacher's attention to an unrelated subject.

Satan isn't above tricks himself. If he can divert human attention to seemingly "good" creatures and away from God Almighty, then he can successfully derail someone's spiritual life. Angels are created beings. They are not the Creator, and they are not to be worshiped. And yet many people find it easier to believe in guardian angels, as if they're some good luck charm, rather than to believe in God Himself.

Colossians 2:18-19 tells us to beware anyone who teaches the worship of angels. "Let no one disqualify you, insisting on asceticism and worship of angels, going on in detail about visions, puffed up without reason by his sensuous mind, and not holding fast to the Head, from whom the whole body, nourished and knit together through its joints and ligaments, grows with a growth that is from God." The early church must have faced the same temptation we face today—the temptation to lose our focus on the Creator and settle for something or someone created.

Same old trick. The redirect.

Read Today's Scripture:
Hebrews 1:5-9 and Revelation 22:8-9

1. What does Hebrews 1:5-9 say about Jesus and the angels?

   _____

   _____

   _____

   _____

2. What was the angel's response to John in Revelation 22:8-9?

   _____

   _____

   _____

   _____

3. How does the world view angels? What do these verses teach us about the correct view of angels?

   _____

   _____

   _____

   _____

Today's Journal:

Do you sense the Holy Spirit applying these scriptures to your own life? Has Satan ever tricked you into redirecting your worship? Explain.

_____

_____

_____

_____

_____

_____

_____

_____

_____

_____

_____

_____

_____

Day 3. Jesus, the Alpha and Omega

In the beginning was the Word, and the Word was with God, and the Word was God. He was in the beginning with God. All things were made through him, and without him was not any thing made that was made.

John 1:1-3

Genesis is hotly debated among Christians today. Christians are divided. Some believe in a young-earth creation (YC) with six literal 24-hour days of creation; others believe in an old-earth creation (OC) with each day of creation being longer than 24 hours or being non-consecutive. According to Ted Cabal in the *Apologetics Study Bible*, "Some YCs accuse OCs of compromising the Bible with evolutionary science. Some OCs charge YCs with undermining biblical credibility by generating a false conflict between science and the Scriptures."[7]

Though the battle for the beginning will continue, we must agree on this: Jesus was there before it all began.

Jesus is everlasting. He was with God in the beginning, but He Himself has no beginning because He is God. This is a central truth. The supremacy of Christ is established in the book of Hebrews, and it is confirmed for us in John 1:1-3. Jesus isn't just a worthy cause or some spiritual guide. He is God in human form. Without Him, we wouldn't exist. "For in Him we live and move and have our being" (Acts 17:28a).

Jesus was with God in the beginning, and He'll be with God in the end. "Therefore God exalted him to the highest place and gave him the name that is above every name, that at the name of Jesus every knee should bow, in heaven and on earth and under the earth, and every tongue confess that Jesus Christ is Lord, to the glory of God the Father" (Philippians 2:9-11 NIV). His supremacy is secure. He is from everlasting to everlasting. He doesn't exist because of someone else; He is the self-existent One. This places Him above every other prophet, real or otherwise, on the planet.

Read Today's Scripture:
Hebrews 1:10-14 and Revelation 1:8, 17

1. Why is it important to understand that Jesus has no beginning and no end?

2. If you believed that Jesus was another created being, how might that affect your faith and your life as a Christian?

3. According to the Blackabys in their Hebrews study guide, "He who creates, owns."[8] What does that phrase mean to you?

Today's Journal:

Is the Lord applying these verses to your life in any way as He challenges you to develop a faith that endures? How does the fact that Jesus is the Alpha and Omega affect your daily life?

Day 4. Jesus, Our Salvation

See then that you walk circumspectly, not as fools but as wise.
Ephesians 5:15 (NKJV)

Where was that steeple? The stone buildings surrounding me hid St. Stephens Cathedral, and I could no longer see the cross that was visible just moments ago. Earlier that day, my friend and I had arrived in Austria on different flights, so we agreed to meet at the steps of the historic landmark. "Just look for the beautiful Gothic church in the center of Vienna," she told me. Looking out of my hotel window, I could see the church spire towering over the city, so off I went. But once I was in the city center, the once-prominent steeple promptly vanished.

I wandered down a cobblestone street in search of the famous church. Drifting past cafés, I saw folks sipping coffee and speaking rapidly in German. Though I hoped for an English-speaking passerby, I found no one. I started to panic. What if I couldn't find my friend? Worse yet, what if I couldn't find my way back to the hotel?

That wasn't the first time I'd been lost—I often lose my way. When driving, I get lost because I rarely look out my side windows and note the changing landscape. When walking, I fail to notice my surroundings and end up disoriented. In short, simple journeys become adventures because I don't pay attention.

In our walk with Christ, we are warned to pay attention: to treat the object of our attention with care. The writer of Hebrews promises that when we take note of our situation, we will not drift away (Hebrews 2:1).

Now I pay more careful attention when I read my Bible and pray. I pay attention to God's prompting in my heart. Though I may continue to wander through life's streets, I want to look up and find His steeple. I want to focus on God so that I don't drift away from the path He has laid out for me.

Read Today's Scripture:
Hebrews 2:1-4 and Luke 2:8-20

1. In what ways could we "ignore so great a salvation"?

   _____

   _____

   _____

   _____

2. What names does the passage in Luke give to Jesus? Which of those names is most meaningful to you? Why?

   _____

   _____

   _____

   _____

3. Since our salvation has a name, can you add any further insight to your answer to the first question above? What most often prompts you to "ignore so great a salvation"?

   _____

   _____

   _____

   _____

Today's Journal:

How do today's scriptures encourage you to strengthen your faith? Have you ever drifted from God's path? What do you do to stay focused on God?

Day 5. Jesus Succeeded Where Adam Failed

But we see him who for a little while was made lower than the angels, namely Jesus, crowned with glory and honor because of the suffering of death, so that by the grace of God he might taste death for everyone.

Hebrews 2:9

Satan tempted Eve with beautiful, tasty fruit that was off-limits. He made it sound even more appealing by reminding her how wise she'd be if she ate it. How exciting the power of knowledge would be if she could have just one bite.

When Adam and Eve sinned, they failed in three ways: (1) the food would fill their stomachs, (2) the fruit looked beautiful, and (3) it promised to make them wise "like gods." "So when the woman saw that the tree was good for food, and that it was a delight to the eyes, and that the tree was to be desired to make one wise, she took of its fruit and ate, and she also gave some to her husband who was with her, and he ate" (Genesis 3:6). So there they are—the three big culprits. "For all that is in the world, the lust of the flesh, and the lust of the eyes, and the pride of life, is not of the Father, but is of the world" (1 John 2:16 KJV). Thus, Adam sinned and we've been under sin's curse ever since.

Jesus never sinned. He was "tempted as we are," but He didn't fail (Hebrews 4:15). When Satan tempted Jesus in Luke 4:1-12, he appealed to Jesus' hunger. Not succeeding in tripping up Jesus with the lust of the flesh, Satan turned to the lust of the eyes: "And the devil took him up and showed him all the kingdoms of the world…" (Luke 4:5). Finally, Satan tried the pride of life: "If you are the Son of God, throw yourself down from here" (Luke 4:9). Jesus was able to thwart Satan's plan. He succeeded where Adam had failed, and thereby rescued us from the curse of sin. Our sin, inherited from Adam, has forced us into a debt that we can never repay (Romans 5:19). Jesus, our champion, is the only one righteous enough to pay the debt and rescue us from the trap of sin. One man tasted death so that all may live.

Read Today's Scripture:
Hebrews 2:5-9 and Romans 5:15-21

1. What does Hebrews 2:5-9 say about man in relation to the rest of creation?

   _____

   _____

   _____

   _____

2. How does Romans 5:15-21 improve your understanding of the passage in Hebrews above?

   _____

   _____

   _____

   _____

Today's Journal:
Jesus freed you from the penalty of sin. What impact does that have on your faith?

Final Thoughts

> *Once you are rooted in reality, nothing can shake you. If your faith is in experiences, anything that happens is likely to upset that faith. But nothing can ever change God or the reality of redemption. Base your faith on that, and you are as eternally secure as God Himself.*
>
> Oswald Chambers[9]

Sometimes I catch myself thinking, *If I have this one thing, I'll be all right.* This one thing can be a home, a family, my health. *I may face financial struggles, but as long as I have a roof over my head, I'll be all right.* Or *I may lose my job, but as long as I have my health, I'll be all right.* These thoughts slip in when I'm trying to look on the bright side of a dark situation. When I'm trying to be optimistic.

But that "one thing" will never be reliable. Only Jesus is.

Jesus is superior. Faith in anyone or anything else will crumble. Though the world around us looks for hope in political leaders, the economy, or the environment, our hope is in Christ alone. Our faith does not rest on man's wisdom, but on God's power (1 Corinthians 2:5). This week's study reminds us that Jesus is indeed the Superior One. The only sure foundation for our faith. People of faith are rooted in the reality of that truth.

Week 2.
Jesus Invites Us To Cease from Our Works and Enter His Rest

She balanced plates on the sticks in her hands, on her forehead, and in her mouth. To keep the plates in the air, the petite Chinese performer had to keep them spinning. On stage in Beijing, with her body twisting like a rubber band, she magically kept all the plates in place. We watched with anticipation as they whirled. If one of them slowed down, even for an instant, it would come crashing to the ground and ruin her performance.

Some time ago, I saw a brochure for a Christian women's conference that began with "Attention all plate spinners…" I knew it was talking to me. In more than one season of life, I've felt like that acrobat balancing spinning plates on the ends of sticks. Make one more phone call, complete one more project, cross one more item off my list. If any one thing is ignored, everything might come crashing down and ruin my performance. It all depends on me, doesn't it?

Wrong. It doesn't depend on me at all. It depends on Christ and what He has completed on my behalf. In Luke 10, Martha was busy preparing a meal and wearing herself out in the process. Fix one more dish, finish one more task—why is no one helping me? But Jesus noted that Mary had made the wiser choice to sit at His feet and listen. Likewise, Jesus invites us to enter His Sabbath rest and trust His work on our behalf.

Working hard to earn Jesus' approval is a natural tendency. If I make a mistake, I feel unworthy of His love. When I do well, I'm tempted to pat myself on the back and enjoy a moment of spiritual pride. God's Word teaches us that works never earn God's approval. Our best efforts will never be enough—in fact, they are nothing more than "filthy rags" in His sight (Isaiah 64:6 NIV). Salvation is not earned; it is accepted. Jesus paid our sin debt in full when He died on the cross; therefore, we can quit trying to earn His approval or the approval of other people. We can rest. This week, we'll study the rest into which we're invited to enter. Let's stop spinning our plates and enter His Sabbath rest.

Day 1. Our Kinsman Redeemer

Since therefore the children share in flesh and blood, he himself likewise partook of the same things, that through death he might destroy the one who has the power of death, that is, the devil, and deliver all those who through fear of death were subject to lifelong slavery.

Hebrews 2:14-15

Hopeless. Hungry. No backup plan.

Two lonely widows—Naomi and her daughter-in-law, Ruth—have nothing left. No relatives willing to support them. No alternative but to return to Naomi's Hebrew homeland.

Leaving Moab, they return to Naomi's former home, Bethlehem, but they need to be rescued from their poverty by a family member, the next of kin. If the kinsman redeemer is willing to buy back their family land and take responsibility for the women, they will be saved (Leviticus 25:25-34).

Boaz, a relative who undertakes Ruth and Naomi's cause, offers the opportunity to serve as the kinsman redeemer to the nearest kin: "If you will redeem it, do so. But if you will not, let me know. For no one has the right to do it except you, and I am next in line" (Ruth 4:4 NIV).

When the nearest kin chooses not to redeem the property, Boaz steps in and saves the women. Ruth's story is told in the Old Testament book that bears her name. She is an outsider from Moab, but she and Naomi are rescued by Boaz, their kinsman redeemer. "The women said to Naomi: 'Praise be to the Lord, who this day has not left you without a kinsman-redeemer'" (Ruth 4:14 NIV).

Like Ruth and Naomi, we too are trapped, without hope of rescue. But like Ruth, we have a kinsman redeemer, Jesus, who is the only one able to redeem us. He is willing to save us. Just as Boaz loved Ruth and freed her from a life of poverty, Jesus saw us, loved us, and paid the price to deliver us from the hopelessness of lifelong bondage to sin.

Read Today's Scripture:
Hebrews 2:10-18, Ruth 2–4, and Leviticus 25:25-34

1. Based on Hebrews 2:10-18, how is Jesus our kinsman redeemer?

2. According to Leviticus 25:25-34, what is the role of the kinsman redeemer?

3. What similarities do you see between Boaz as Ruth's kinsman redeemer and Jesus as our kinsman redeemer?

Today's Journal:

What is your response to what you read today? Have you gained any new insight based on these passages? How does Ruth's relationship with her kinsman redeemer strengthen your faith?

Day 2. The House That Christ Built

> *For by grace you have been saved through faith. And this is not your own doing; it is the gift of God, not a result of works, so that no one may boast. For we are his workmanship, created in Christ Jesus for good works, which God prepared beforehand, that we should walk in them.*
>
> Ephesians 2:8-10

The "dancing house" raised quite a stir in Prague when it was completed in 1996. In the midst of the traditional baroque and gothic architecture of this historic city, the dancing house stands in sharp contrast with its curved walls that appear to be frozen mid-spin. The Czech people finally adjusted to the newness of it all, and today tourists flock to the famous workmanship of architects Vlado Milonic and Frank Gehry.[10]

Like the steel and concrete of a building, a lump of clay—unformed and unfunctional—will never become beautiful or useful on its own. It needs a potter. The clay has no right to question the potter's motive or method. It is the created thing, not the creator.

> You turn things upside down!
> Shall the potter be regarded as the clay,
> that the thing made should say of its maker,
> "He did not make me";
> or the thing formed say of him who formed it,
> "He has no understanding"? (Isaiah 29:16)

The potter has a vision of what the clay will become, and with expertise that is his alone, he patiently shapes the clay into an object of value.

Every masterpiece begins with the design of the master builder. Clay needs a sculptor. A house needs a builder. Once formed, a sculpture brings glory to its artist and a house brings glory to its architect. We admire the vision and expertise of an expert when we see an object's usefulness and appreciate its beauty.

Today's passage in Hebrews describes us—the body of believers—as the house that Christ built. His workmanship. Moses was worthy of honor, but he was only a member of God's household. The true architect and builder is God Himself. The real honor goes to Jesus.

Read Today's Scripture:
Hebrews 3:1-6 and 1 Corinthians 6:19-20

1. What does Hebrews 3:6 mean to you? What additional insight can you glean from 1 Corinthians 6:19-20?

   _____

   _____

   _____

   _____

2. How can the truths from these passages influence how we behave on a daily basis? How can they influence our ministry and role in the local church?

   _____

   _____

   _____

   _____

Today's Journal:

What is God saying to you personally today about faith that endures? In what ways are you a "faithful son over God's house?"

Day 3. A Time of Testing

> *Therefore, as the Holy Spirit says, "Today, if you hear his voice, do not harden your hearts as in the rebellion, on the day of testing in the wilderness.*
>
> Hebrews 3:7-8

"Come here," I called out.

"Why?" my son replied.

"Doesn't matter why. I said, come here!"

Rather than run straight over to me, he first wanted to know if he was going to like my answer. But what if the reason I called him over was serious? At the ripe old age of five, was he in any position to decide whether or not he should come to me immediately? He didn't know what I knew. He couldn't see what I could see. He had no way of knowing whether he was in danger or if I had called him over simply to give him a hug. His delay could have come at great cost.

Over the years, my husband and I have tried to teach our kids that delayed obedience is disobedience. Partial obedience is also disobedience. Furthermore, resentful obedience—full of murmuring and complaining—is disobedience too. True obedience is immediate, complete, and cheerful. Our kids, like all kids, have not always chosen full obedience.

Part of teaching children to grow into responsible, mature adults is insisting on full obedience in circumstances where they find it difficult to obey. Will they choose to turn off the television immediately when I call their names, or will they delay until it's more convenient for them? Will they complete their chores or will they rush through them haphazardly? Will they cheerfully submit when we say they can't participate in an activity with their friends? The choice is theirs. They can submit to our training and mature, or they can harden their hearts and miss the opportunity to be blessed.

The Israelites didn't always choose full obedience either, and God wasn't impressed with their murmuring and complaining. He called it a "hardened heart." We are to learn from their example so that we don't develop a hardened heart.

Read Today's Scripture:
Hebrews 3:7-11 and Deuteronomy 8:2-3

1. The time that the Israelites spent in the desert is described as a "time of testing." What reasons are given in Deuteronomy 8:2-3 for this testing?

2. Based on Hebrews 3:7-11, did the Israelites pass the test? What was God's response to the Israelites?

Today's Journal:

How can you apply these same warnings to your own life of faith? Are you experiencing a time of testing in your life right now? How are you responding?

Day 4. Sin's Deceitfulness

But exhort one another every day, as long as it is called "today," that none of you may be hardened by the deceitfulness of sin.

Hebrews 3:13

Several years ago, Hollywood made a film about a child adopted by a movie production company. In *The Truman Show* starring Jim Carrey,[11] the boy was raised on the set for the television show and never knew that his "parents" were paid actors. His neighbors and friends were extras. Each day he walked down the street and greeted people that were paid to greet him in return. Then one day his eyes were opened. Instead of his perfect home and neighborhood, he saw an artificial main street. Rather than family and friends, he saw hired hands. His world, as enticing as it was, came to an end when he discovered the edge of the movie set and climbed out.

Sin is tricky. Like a movie set of a neighborly main street with beckoning storefront windows and inviting front doors, sin is an attractive façade. Look closely, however, and we find that nothing is for sale in the store, and no one lives behind those front doors. Sin is a charade, a mirage, a trick. It is never what it seems.

Not only does sin trick us into believing it is desirable, it has a secondary effect as well. Sin causes us to turn away from God. Whenever I've toyed with a pet sin, I've found myself uncomfortable in church. Believers irritate me. I'm critical of the preaching and the choir stops sounding good. I think I can walk away from my sin anytime I'm ready. Then, one day I wake up to find myself tangled in sin's deceitfulness. Nothing short of the power of God can free me.

Read Today's Scripture:
Hebrews 3:12-19, Galatians 6:1-3, and 1 Corinthians 10:11-13

1. What warnings are we given in Hebrews 3:12-19?

   _____

   _____

   _____

   _____

2. What further warnings and instructions are we given in Galatians 6:1-3?

   _____

   _____

   _____

   _____

3. What encouragement can you gain from 1 Corinthians 10:11-13?

   _____

   _____

   _____

   _____

Today's Journal:

Without revealing too many details, can you give an example of sin's deceitfulness in your own life? How do you respond to the encouragement found in today's scriptures?

_____

_____

_____

_____

_____

_____

_____

_____

_____

_____

_____

Day 5. Sabbath Rest

So then, there remains a Sabbath rest for the people of God, for whoever has entered God's rest has also rested from his works as God did from his.

Hebrews 4:9-10

Giggling, the kids gripped the mallet and tried to guess where the mole's head would pop up next.

"Quick, thump him on the head."

"Oh no! There, you missed him."

"Faster. Faster. There's another one. And another."

"You're too slow!"

The Whack-a-Mole game at the county fair is a crowd-pleaser. Each time the mole pops out of the hole, you pound him on the head with a mallet. You win by whacking the moles just as quickly as they appear. Unfortunately, they appear faster than you can whack them, and in the end you discover you just aren't fast enough.

At a young age, when I first became conscious of my shortcomings, I tried to do better. Each time I slipped up, I felt guilty and promised not to do it again. No matter how hard I tried, I found myself repeating sins. I lived in a cycle of promises followed by frustration. Like the mole in the game, sin appeared faster than I could whack it on the head.

We all respond to the Holy Spirit's flashlight on our lives in different ways. Some of us immediately see our need for Christ, abandon our old lives, and follow Jesus. Others of us first try to get our act together before we realize that our best efforts aren't good enough. Jesus is not impressed by our efforts or our promises to do better. No amount of rededication will change the fact that sin can't be defeated by trying harder. Instead, Jesus invites us to rest. "Come unto me" is His offer in Matthew 11. There exists, therefore, a Sabbath rest for the people of God where we cease from our own works and trust in His finished work on our behalf.

Read Today's Scripture:
Hebrews 4:1-11 and Matthew 11:28-30

1. What lessons can we learn from the Israelites who "formerly had the gospel preached to them?"

2. What do you think the writer of Hebrews means by a Sabbath rest for the people of God? How is it an act of unbelief to refuse to enter into His rest?

3. Many people view Christianity as bondage with a list of rules to follow. How does the invitation in Matthew 11:28-30 refute that viewpoint?

Today's Journal:

Can you share a testimony about experiencing God's rest in your life? What most often keeps you from living by faith and enjoying the rest God offers?

Final Thoughts

Ask a teenager, "How are you?" and the most likely answer you'll receive is, "I'm tired." College students and adults too. Young or old, we're tired. Physically run down from long days and sleepless nights. Emotionally worn out from worry. Spiritually exhausted from trying to please others. Just plain tired.

According to a national study, an estimated 50 to 70 million Americans report ongoing sleep problems: not enough sleep, sleep at the wrong time, or poor quality sleep. Sleep deficiency has been linked to heart disease, kidney disease, high blood pressure, diabetes, stroke, obesity, and depression.[12] Our health suffers without sleep. Our relationships also suffer. Too often I've snapped at my kids just because I was tired. And how many poor decisions could I have avoided if I had just been more rested? Sleepiness has led to cloudy judgment and countless accidents, some of them tragic. Contrary to popular opinion, we can't learn to get by on less sleep.

Are you spiritually tired? Maybe you've worked hard to please God and others, but find the heaviness of sin exhausting. If the burden you're carrying has worn you out, Jesus' invitation is "come unto Me." Just come. In Him, you'll find the rest you need.

Jesus is our kinsman redeemer and our master sculptor. He brings life where sin generates death. He brings peace where turmoil reigns. Our message this week is one of hope. It is also a reminder to turn away from the deceitfulness of sin so that our hearts won't be hardened. Instead, find rest in Christ alone. His Sabbath rest is available for all of us plate-spinners. Let's stop playing Whack-a-Sin and enter His promised rest.

Week 3.

Jesus Grants Us Access to the Throne of Grace

The business world has a new word for top managers: C-level Executives. They're the top brass with "Chief" in their titles: Chief Executive Officer (CEO), Chief Financial Officer (CFO), Chief Operating Officer (COO). Gaining access to the C-suite is nearly impossible. The mahogany-lined corner offices are off-limits to most of us. C-level executives usually have administrative assistants who serve as gatekeepers; they screen all calls and determine which ones get attention. The assistants often have tremendous power because they have the authority to give visitors access to the CEO.

Not long ago, as I was preparing to speak to a class about commercial banks, I stumbled across a question I couldn't answer. I tried to research it on my own, but I knew the best answer would come from a real live bank president. So I called a local bank president with my question. His secretary answered the phone, took my message, and I assumed that would be the end of that. What bank president has time to return my call? If I was lucky, maybe my question would be passed down to a lower level employee, but he probably wouldn't call me back either.

To my surprise, the bank president returned my call within twenty-four hours. Can you believe it? Trust me, nothing about my message was impressive enough to grab his attention. I simply had a question, and he kindly answered it.

More powerful than the most important bank president is our God who invites us to come boldly before His throne. He grants us access that we otherwise would not have. Jesus is both the CEO and the gatekeeper. We can walk straight into that mahogany-lined corner office unannounced. No appointment. No secretary to screen our calls. No closed office door. Jesus invites us into a personal relationship and offers us a future and a hope. "Let us then with confidence draw near to the throne of grace, that we may receive mercy and find grace to help in time of need" (Hebrews 4:16).

Day 1. The Living, Active Word of God

For the word of God is living and active, sharper than any two-edged sword, piercing to the division of soul and of spirit, of joints and of marrow, and discerning the thoughts and intentions of the heart.

Hebrews 4:12

Each semester, university students are given an end-of-term questionnaire to evaluate the quality of the course and the effectiveness of the professor. Was the course difficult or easy? Did the teacher provide clear explanations? Was the professor accessible during office hours? And one more question: what grade do you expect to earn in this course?

My students complete these student evaluations each semester, and the answers to the last question tell me quite a lot. The A student is likely to give high marks to a challenging professor, while the F student is likely to praise an easy professor. Funny thing is, though, I can't remember the last time I saw an evaluation where the student expected to earn a C, D, or an F. And yet, students do earn Cs, Ds, and Fs with some regularity.

So maybe the questionnaire isn't as enlightening as I envision. In terms of human behavior, this question is an eye-opener: "what grade do you expect?" It shows that we humans don't evaluate ourselves accurately. Many of us give ourselves the benefit of the doubt. We hope for, maybe even expect, an A or a B at the end of the day. In fact, we're pretty sure we're above average.

You may say, "No, that's not me. I'm no A student. I'm the worst of the worst." Rather than an overly optimistic view of yourself, you see nothing but flaws. A collection of blunders. Where others see themselves as above average in skill, you see yourself as above average in mistakes. Sin that can't be erased. Ugliness that can't be restored.

Reality, however, often tells an entirely different story.

God's Word is the great revealer. We may be blind to our true condition, but nothing is hidden from the Lord. When we read the Bible, our secret motives become clear. We see who God is, and then the spotlight is turned on us so that we can see who we are as well. "All are naked and exposed to the eyes of him to whom we must give account" (Hebrews 4:13).

So what grade are you hoping to receive?

I've discovered that the Bible brings into proper perspective those things that make me squirm and those things that tempt me to be prideful. It allows me to see that the grade I *deserve* is not the grade that I should *expect*. Due to my sinfulness, I've earned an F, but it's been erased. God's mercy has given me the grade that Jesus earned. An A.

Read Today's Scripture:
Hebrews 4:12-13, Ephesians 6:17, and Psalm 119:105, 129-130

1. How does Hebrews 4:12-13 describe God's Word? How does Ephesians 6:17 describe the Word of God?

   _____

   _____

   _____

   _____

2. What do Psalm 119:105, 129-130 say about the Word of God?

   _____

   _____

   _____

   _____

3. Describe a time in your life when God's Word gave you light and understanding.

   _____

   _____

   _____

   _____

Today's Journal:

What are you battling today? How can God's Word be your sword as you develop a faith that endures?

Day 2. Jesus, Our Great High Priest
> *For we do not have a high priest who is unable to sympathize with our weaknesses, but one who in every respect has been tempted as we are, yet without sin.*
>
> Hebrews 4:15

What makes us uniquely human? Our physical bodies, our emotions and personalities, our family relationships, and more.

Jesus experienced all this. Everything that defines humanity could be found in Him—everything except sin, that is. He was "tempted as we are" according to Hebrews 4:15. He didn't have to experience the physical pain that comes with having a body. He could have avoided the tears He experienced when His friend Lazarus died. He could have done without the betrayal of friends if He had refused to become a man. He was God Himself, after all, and He could have skipped the suffering that we experience.

But He didn't skip any of it. "Although he was a son, He learned obedience through what He suffered" (Hebrews 5:8). The Greek word for "learn" means to experience something firsthand, and by experience to make it one's own. Jesus experienced everything we experience, and He willingly made it His own.

Though He became man and suffered like us, He never sinned. That one fact makes Him the only one qualified to serve as our High Priest and to speak to the Father on our behalf. He is the only one who was tempted in every way and yet never succumbed to the temptation. Therefore, we're invited to "with confidence draw near to the throne of grace" (Hebrews 4:16).

Confidence without arrogance. Understanding that we can be bold but not brazen. We have the wonderful privilege of an intercessor who was not just a mortal man. He is God in the flesh. Let us accept His invitation and approach the throne of grace today.

Read Today's Scripture:
Hebrews 4:14-5:10 and Romans 8:31-39

1. Based on Hebrews 4:14-5:10, how does having Jesus as our High Priest help us?

2. According to Hebrews 4:16, what does it mean to "draw near to the throne of grace" with confidence?

3. According to Romans 8:31-39, Christ is interceding for us today. What benefits does Christ's intercession bring to the believer?

Today's Journal:

Can you describe a time when you came boldly to the throne of grace and obtained mercy in your time of need? What faith is required when we approach the Lord in prayer?

Day 3. Milk or Meat?

For everyone who lives on milk is unskilled in the word of righteousness, since he is a child. But solid food is for the mature, for those who have their powers of discernment trained by constant practice to distinguish good from evil.

Hebrews 5:13-14

We bought a set of bunk beds when our kids were young. The men came to deliver the bed, and after they finished assembling it, one of them warned the kids not to jump on the bed. He told them, "This bed contains an alarm that will sound at our store if you jump on the bed. If we hear the alarm, we'll come and take the bed away."

Sometime later, our six-year-old daughter pulled me aside. "Mommy," she said, "I don't think the alarm is working. We jumped on the bed, but no one came to take it away." She had no reason to think that the deliverymen would lie to her. She wasn't old enough to see through their story. I had overheard the men and knew they were kidding, but it never occurred to me that the kids would take the warning to heart.

One mark of maturity is the ability to discern truth from fiction and right from wrong—not being "carried about with every wind of doctrine" (Ephesians 4:14 KJV). The more time we spend getting to know God and understanding His Word, the more quickly we're able to see when an idea doesn't quite line up with what God says. Today's reading challenges us to grow up. There's work to be done. It's time to get out of the nursery.

Read Today's Scripture:
Hebrews 5:11-6:3 and Ephesians 4:14-16

1. What are some of the differences between infants and grown-ups in Hebrews 5:11-14 and Ephesians 4:14-16?

2. What does Paul list as 'elementary teachings' in Hebrews 6:1-3?

3. Can you think of any examples in your own life or in the lives of other believers where you've seen evidence of spiritual maturity?

Today's Journal:

Take a few minutes to respond to what God has shown you today. Perhaps you can write a prayer asking God for the discernment that comes with spiritual maturity as you strengthen your faith.

Day 4. The Good Soil

For land that has drunk the rain that often falls on it, and produces a crop useful to those for whose sake it is cultivated, receives a blessing from God.

Hebrews 6:7

Two rosebushes live in my garden—one on either side of my front porch. One is bushy, full of fragrant pink-red roses. The other is small, stilted, thin, with only an occasional bud to remind me it really is a rosebush. Why the difference?

Both plants receive the same sunshine, rain, and fertilizer. Both are subject to the same pruning, and yet they produce entirely different results. On the outside, I can't see any reason for the difference, so it must be something I can't see: the roots and the soil. The healthy bush must have healthy roots in good soil, roots that can extract the nutrients from the soil. The sickly rosebush must have shallow or shriveled roots in poor soil. Unable to be nourished, the plant is unable to produce beautiful roses.

God sows the seed of His Word in hearts. Some hearts are receptive; others are not. A heart that comes in contact with the Word of God and remains unchanged produces nothing. Though touched by God's Word, it is not truly converted. That heart may appear healthy for a season, but soon it withers. Eventually, it looks nothing like the bushy, fragrant, fruitful heart with healthy roots and beautiful flowers.

But for some, God's Word takes root and produces a beautiful crop of blessing. If our hearts are receptive, His Word will change our perspective. From the outside, others will see the difference. They may not understand the difference, but they'll see the roses and they'll notice the fragrance. "But thanks be to God, who in Christ always leads us in triumphal procession, and through us spreads the fragrance of the knowledge of him everywhere. For we are the aroma of Christ to God among those who are being saved and among those who are perishing" (2 Corinthians 2:14-15).

Read Today's Scripture:
Hebrews 6:4-12 and Matthew 13:1-9, 18-23

1. According to Hebrews 6:4-12, how might we crucify "once again the Son of God" if we reject Him?

2. According to Matthew 13:1-9 and 18-23, what are the four possible responses to God's Word?

3. What lessons are there in these passages for us? How can we apply these lessons to ourselves and to our churches?

Today's Journal:

What is the soil of your heart like—stony, thorny, shallow, or fertile?

Day 5. Behind the Curtain

But now in Christ Jesus you who once were far off have been brought near by the blood of Christ.

Ephesians 2:13

A heavy curtain, inches thick, almost a wall, separates the space and says, "This far and no farther." The strongest have tried to muscle in. The smartest, the fastest, the sweetest—they all try but the curtain remains in place. A barrier exists between God and man.

All religions work hard to tear away the curtain, but no amount of effort is ever enough. Deep down, we all know that if we can just remove the barrier, we'll find peace. But real peace is only found in a relationship with Jesus. He's the only one who can bring us into contact with God. Christ alone gives us hope. He is the One who can take us behind the curtain.

In the Old Testament tabernacle, a veil—a curtain—separated the Holy Place from the Most Holy Place (Exodus 26:33). Only the high priest could enter the inner sanctuary once a year on the Day of Atonement (Leviticus 16). Common people? Never. Non-Jews? Absolutely not.

When Jesus died on the cross, an amazing thing happened. From top to bottom, the veil was torn in two. Finally, we were invited into a personal, intimate relationship with God Himself.

Read Today's Scripture:
Hebrews 6:13-20, Matthew 27:51, and 2 Corinthians 3:12-18

1. According to Matthew 27:51, what happened to the temple curtain the day that Jesus died on the cross? What do you think that symbolizes for us?

2. What is the veil described in 2 Corinthians 3:12-18 and what does it represent? How is this veil removed?

3. How would you describe the "hope" in Hebrews 6:18-19 that you now have as a Christian?

Today's Journal:

What is your response to what you read today? Do you have a testimony of a time in your life when Jesus offered you hope that served as an anchor for your soul? How does that experience encourage you as you develop a faith that endures?

_____

_____

_____

_____

_____

_____

_____

_____

_____

Final Thoughts

I always shudder when a child calls me by my first name. It's a cultural thing—maybe even a teacher thing. I was raised with Mister and Miss, and I've raised my own kids that way. Different countries have different attitudes towards formality. Some consider the use of titles respectful; others think it's stuffy and pretentious.

In business, the gap between boss and employee is called the Power Distance.[13] A low power distance exists when people communicate on a first-name basis and junior employees can easily approach senior management. A high power distance is just the opposite. Always formal, never at ease.

Living in a low power distance culture, I sometimes have trouble focusing on the greatness of our God. Church becomes commonplace, and prayer is taken lightly. In this week's study, I was reminded that Christ alone has the authority and the ability to step behind the veil. In Him, I'm invited to approach a holy God in the most holy place. The gap is filled; the power distance no longer exists. Only reverence and awe remain.

He invites us to enjoy His presence. Come, approach God's throne with boldness. The invitation is open. And as we grow as Christians, may God's Word take root in our hearts so that we may be the aroma of Christ to the outside world. Cultivate a faith that endures.

Week 4.
Jesus, Our High Priest, Is Able To Completely Save Us

Not just anyone could be a priest in Israel. When God established His covenant with Moses, He specified that priests must be descendants of Levi, the third of Jacob's twelve sons. The priests had to be qualified.

One priest, however, was mentioned in the Old Testament long before there were Levitical priests. That priest is Melchizedek and he's a mystery. We have no record of his beginning or his end. And though the qualifications for priesthood were not yet written, somehow, Abraham knew that Melchizedek had met God's requirements.

Not all priests throughout history were so well qualified. In Ezra's time, some men should never have been made priests in the first place: "These searched for their family records, but they could not find them and so were excluded from the priesthood as unclean" (Ezra 2:62 NIV). In 1 Kings, wicked King Jeroboam selected his own priests, and that greatly displeased God. "Even after this, Jeroboam did not change his evil ways, but once more appointed priests for the high places from all sorts of people. Anyone who wanted to become a priest, he consecrated for the high places. This was the sin of the house of Jeroboam that led to its downfall and to its destruction from the face of the earth" (1 Kings 13:33-34 NIV).

Jesus is the final, qualified high priest. Where others failed, Jesus succeeded. He is qualified because God said so, and Jesus proved He was worthy of that qualification by His sinless character. Where the old, temporary priesthood failed to give people the power to live changed lives, Jesus, our permanent High Priest, is able to completely save us from our sin. In Jesus, God established a new covenant that isn't written on tablets of stone, but rather is written on our hearts (Jeremiah 31:33). Because of Jesus, we who were once far away are now included in the family of God. "But you are a chosen people, a royal priesthood, a holy nation, a people belonging to God, that you may declare the praises of him who called you out of darkness into his wonderful light" (1 Peter 2:9 NIV).

This week in our study of Hebrews, we'll look at the superior priesthood of Jesus. His priesthood is permanent and powerful because He has the power to forgive sins and change lives.

Day 1. The Pre-Priesthood Priest

He is without father or mother or genealogy, having neither beginning of days nor end of life, but resembling the Son of God he continues a priest forever.

Hebrews 7:3

Do you know much about your ancestors? Did you meet your great-grandparents? Has your family lived on the same land for generations?

Many of us are fascinated by our family histories. Knowing those who have gone before us gives us a sense of permanence. Most of the individuals we meet in the Old Testament are identified by their genealogies. Though we may not know much about each man, we usually learn who his father was, who his children were, and how long he lived.

Not so with Melchizedek, the king of Salem who came to meet Abraham after Abraham won a battle. Unlike others in the Bible, Melchizedek's ancestry is never given; neither do we learn anything further about his life. As a man, he had an actual birth and death, but because he appears suddenly, without explanation in the biblical record, it seems that he has no beginning and no end.

Melchizedek is not like the priests we meet later in the Bible because he was both a king and a priest. And unlike the Jewish priests, he was not a member of the Levite tribe. In fact, the twelve tribes of Israel didn't even exist yet. As we'll see in our reading below, Abraham recognized that Melchizedek's authority had been established by God. When Abraham bowed down to this King-Priest, it's as if all of Abraham's descendants were, in effect, paying homage as well.

Like Melchizedek, Jesus was not born into the tribe of Levi—the tribe of priests. Jesus was born into the tribe of Judah, which carried the royal lineage of King David. Jesus, then, is our King-Priest. He is able to approach God because, like Melchizedek's, His authority is established by God Himself.

Read Today's Scripture:
Hebrews 7:1-10, Genesis 14:18, and Psalm 110:4

1. Based on Hebrews 7:1-10 and Genesis 14:18, what evidence do we have that Melchizedek is greater than Abraham?

   _____

   _____

   _____

   _____

2. According to Psalm 110:4, who established Jesus as a priest forever? What does it mean to you that Jesus is your priest forever?

   _____

   _____

   _____

   _____

Today's Journal:

When we pray, we can praise God by thanking Him for who He is. Today, as you reflect on what you read, perhaps you can write a prayer of praise thanking God for who He is according to what He showed you in His Word today. If today's passage was difficult to understand, tell the Lord about it and ask Him to clarify it for you.

Day 2. The Weak Levitical Priesthood

> *Now if perfection (a perfect fellowship between God and the worshiper) had been attainable by the Levitical priesthood—for under it the people were given the Law—why was it further necessary that there should arise another and different kind of Priest, one after the order of Melchizedek, rather than one appointed after the order and rank of Aaron?*
>
> Hebrews 7:11(AMP)

Rules are made to be broken. Cliché, yes, but true nonetheless. Rules show me that I'm breaking the rules, but they do nothing to help me keep them.

The law that God gave Moses was powerless to change lives. According to one Bible commentary, "The Law provided a standard by which a person could evaluate moral condition, but in its weakness it could not provide life and spiritual vigor to anyone. It was merely a diagnostic tool…It served the function of revealing sin (Romans 3:20), but it could not bring perfection. It could only demonstrate imperfection."[14]

That doesn't mean that the law was meaningless and could be disregarded. Paul tells us that if it weren't for the law, he wouldn't have known what sin was. Without the law telling him not to covet, he would never have become conscious of his own covetousness (Romans 7:7-8).

Where the law failed, Christ succeeded. The Levitical priests could only show people that they were slaves to sin; Jesus, the eternal High Priest is able to set people free from the bondage of sin forever. The Levitical priests had to regularly offer animal sacrifices to cover a person's sin, but Jesus' sacrifice was once for all. Powerless to keep the rules on our own, we've been declared righteous because of Jesus Christ's more powerful priesthood.

There is therefore now no condemnation for those who are in Christ Jesus. For the law of the Spirit of life has set you free in Christ Jesus from the law of sin and death. For God has done what the law, weakened by the flesh, could not do. By sending his own Son in the likeness of sinful flesh and for sin, he condemned sin in the flesh, in order that the righteous requirement of the law might be fulfilled in us, who walk not according to the flesh but according to the Spirit.

(Romans 8:1-4)

Read Today's Scripture:
Hebrews 7:11-19 and Romans 3:20

1. Based on Hebrews 7:11, why was there a need for another priest to come?

2. Based on Romans 3:20, can you think of a time in your life when you became conscious of your own sinfulness as you tried to obey God's law?

3. What does Hebrews 7:19 mean to you when it says "a better hope is introduced through which we draw near to God"?

Today's Journal:

What is your response to what God has shown you in His Word? In what way can Jesus, your permanent High Priest, help you develop a faith that endures?

Day 3. Holy, Blameless, Pure

Therefore He is able also to save to the uttermost (completely, perfectly, finally, and for all time and eternity) those who come to God through Him...

Hebrews 7:25 (AMP)

Do you know that in Christ you were saved, you're being saved, and one day you will be saved? Many Bible teachers have followed theologian Lewis Sperry Chafer[15] and explained the three tenses of salvation: past, present, future.

Past tense: "By grace you have been saved" (Ephesians 2:5). I was saved when I accepted that Jesus' death on the cross was for me—a step called justification. His death saved me from the *penalty* of sin. Present tense: "For the word of the cross is folly to those who are perishing, but to us who are being saved it is the power of God" (1 Corinthians 1:18). I am being saved as I shed old habits and learn to think and act in ways that would please God, a process called sanctification. In other words, Jesus is saving me from the *power* of sin over my life. Future tense: "And not only the creation, but we ourselves, who have the firstfruits of the Spirit, groan inwardly as we wait eagerly for adoption as sons, the redemption of our bodies" (Romans 8:23). One day I will be saved when my life here on earth ends and my days in heaven begin. On that day, Jesus will save me from the very *presence* of sin. That final step is what many call glorification.

Jesus has the power and the authority to save us completely. He is qualified to intervene with the Father on our behalf because of His flawless character. Through Moses, God instructed the Jews to make atonement for their sins by offering animals without defect (Numbers 28). Jesus Himself was that "lamb without defect," the perfect Lamb of God. Holy, blameless, and pure. Unstained by sin. Jesus is the only one able to meet our need for a savior—past, present, and future.

Read Today's Scripture:
Hebrews 7:20-28 and 1 Corinthians 1:30

1. In Hebrews 7:20-22, who made the oath that established Jesus as High Priest?

2. Based on Hebrews 7:23-25, how long will Jesus' priesthood last? What does this say about followers of other world religions who claim that they have heard from a prophet or an intercessor in the years since Jesus came to earth?

3. What has Jesus "become to us" according to 1 Corinthians 1:30? What does it mean that Jesus is our "righteousness and sanctification and redemption"?

Today's Journal:

How do you respond to what God is showing you today about faith that endures? Spend some time thanking Jesus for His daily intercession on your behalf and for the complete salvation He has provided.

Day 4. A Shadow of What Is in Heaven

Such [things] are only the shadow of things that are to come, and they have only a symbolic value. But the reality (the substance, the solid fact of what is foreshadowed, the body of it) belongs to Christ.

Colossians 2:17 (AMP)

"I just can't stand church," claimed one young woman, to whom my dear friend responded, "Then how are you ever going to stand heaven?"

When God instructed Moses about building the tabernacle, He was very specific. He gave dimensions, materials, and even the placement of those materials. He specified who could approach Him. He clarified how they must be dressed and how they should prepare themselves to enter His presence. Every aspect of their "church" was predetermined by God Himself. Moses carefully completed everything exactly as the Lord showed him. The book of Exodus ends with Moses placing all items in the tabernacle "as the Lord had commanded him" (Exodus 40:17-33).

Colossians 2:17 reveals that church practices and worship activities are simply a shadow. The Greek word for *shadow* is *skia* and describes an "image or outline cast by an object."[16] This verse also tells us that the reality is found in Christ. This word, *reality*, is the Greek word *soma*, which literally means "body."[17] In other words, the old religious system was just a rough outline of reality. The One who casts the shadow—that is, the One whose body is the actual substance—is Christ Himself.

Concerning human priests, Hebrews 8:5 states, "They serve at a sanctuary that is a copy and shadow of what is in heaven" (NIV). That's why Moses was warned when he was about to build the tabernacle: "See to it that you make everything according to the pattern shown you on the mountain" (Exodus 25:40). We must remember that our worship here on earth is just a copy of what is in heaven for two reasons. First, it reminds us that the world we now see is strictly temporary. Our permanent home is heaven. Second, it reminds us that God is to be approached His way, not in a way invented by man.

Read Today's Scripture:
Hebrews 8:1-6 and Revelation 21:22

1. What does Hebrews 8:1-2 say to you? How does this affect your life as a Christian?

   _____

   _____

   _____

   _____

2. What does Revelation 21:22 say about the temple in heaven?

   _____

   _____

   _____

   _____

Today's Journal:

All true worship goes through Jesus and all true worship points to Jesus. Is there anything that the Holy Spirit is pointing out to you about your prayer life or about how you approach worship today—something that will help you develop a faith that endures?

Day 5. The New Covenant

And he took bread, and when he had given thanks, he broke it and gave it to them, saying, "This is my body, which is given for you. Do this in remembrance of me." And likewise the cup after they had eaten, saying, "This cup that is poured out for you is the new covenant in my blood."

Luke 22:19-20

Marriage is a covenant. My husband and I wear rings as symbols of our promise to love, honor, and cherish each other as long as we both shall live.

Covenants are contracts that describe what the two signers will or won't do. They are the legal promises we make to one another. A number of covenants are recorded in the Old Testament—all of them initiated by God. God made a covenant with Noah in which He promised never again to destroy the earth by flood (Genesis 9:8-11). God made a covenant with Abraham in which He promised that Abraham's descendants would inherit the land (Genesis 15:17-21). God made a covenant with Moses and the Israelites when He gave them the Ten Commandments written on tablets of stone (Exodus 34:27-28). The covenants often required obedience on the part of the people. In all cases, the people were incapable of fulfilling God's requirements.

In Jesus, we see a new covenant. This is a marriage covenant between Christ—the bridegroom—and His church. His promises are not written on tablets of stone this time. Instead, they're written on our hearts (Hebrews 8:10). Now, because of the new covenant, we can develop a faith that endures.

Read Today's Scripture:
Hebrews 8:7-13 and Jeremiah 31:31-34

1. What does Jeremiah 31:31-34 promise the people of God? What are some of the differences between the old covenant and the new covenant?

   _____

   _____

   _____

   _____

2. What does it mean to have the law on your mind and written on your heart?

   _____

   _____

   _____

   _____

3. What is your response to the promise given in Hebrews 8:12?

   _____

   _____

   _____

   _____

Today's Journal:

How important is your relationship with God? Not in general. How important is it to *you*? Are you trusting that Jesus' blood is sufficient to pay for all your sins? Because of Christ's death, are you developing a faith that endures?

Final Thoughts

Frank Abagnale is a brilliant man. This husband and father of three is a leading expert in the field of embezzlement and forgery. A successful speaker and author, he has served as a consultant to the FBI for over thirty-five years. His methods for fraud prevention have been widely adopted by financial institutions around the world.[18]

Though well respected today, Mr. Abagnale didn't begin his career quite so honorably. He started out as a professional impostor. For years, he posed as a pilot and traveled at the airlines' expense, all the while eluding authorities and cashing bad checks. Later, posing as a doctor and a lawyer, he continued his charade. He was eventually captured and brought to justice. You may know his story because he became the inspiration for the movie, *Catch Me If You Can*.

Frank Abagnale is clearly intelligent, but he is not a pilot. Neither is he a doctor nor a lawyer. No uniform can substitute for real credentials. Credentials are credentials. Training, licensing, certifications—these are the qualifications that make pilots, doctors, and lawyers. Without them, young Frank was just playacting.

Jesus is the real deal. His credentials are impeccable; He's qualified and He's superior. Because He did what no human priest was able to do, He is able to save us completely. Jesus offers us a new covenant, making it possible for us to have a faith that endures.

Week 5.

Jesus, the Superior and Final Sacrifice

I can't stand watching my kids be mean to one another. Of all the ways they can get in trouble, hurting one another is the one that upsets me most. So when my kids were little, I demanded that they apologize to each other. "Say you're sorry," I insisted.

With a scowl, one would reply, "Sorry."

"Now say you're sorry like you mean it!"

"Sooorrry! There."

What I really desired was repentance. I wanted my child to *feel* sorry. After all, when I felt sorry, I asked for forgiveness. And as a young Christian, I thought that was the reason Jesus forgave me. I've since learned I wasn't entirely right.

We should be sorry when we sin. That's the "godly grief" described in 2 Corinthians 7:10. But that's not why we're forgiven. We shortchange others if we suggest that feeling sorry for sin is enough. The real message is the one preached by Paul in 1 Corinthians 1:18, 22-23:

> For the word of the cross is folly to those who are perishing, but to us who are being saved it is the power of God…For Jews demand signs and Greeks seek wisdom, but we preach Christ crucified.

Christ crucified.

This week we'll learn that more important than the message of Jesus' deliverance and healing, and more important than the encouragement for Christians to live godly lives, is the message of Christ crucified. We aren't forgiven because we're really sorry. Neither are we forgiven because we promise we'll do better. We're forgiven because Christ died for our sins. In *My Utmost for His Highest*, Oswald Chambers writes,

> We trample the blood of the Son of God underfoot if we think we are forgiven because we are sorry for our sins. The only reason for the forgiveness of our sins by God, and the infinite depth of His promise to forget them, is the death of Jesus Christ. Our repentance is merely the result of our personal realization of the atonement by the Cross of Christ, which He has provided for us.[19]

Day 1. The First Tabernacle

Seeing that that first [outer portion of the] tabernacle was a parable (a visible symbol or type or picture of the present age). In it gifts and sacrifices are offered, and yet are incapable of perfecting the conscience or of cleansing and renewing the inner man of the worshiper.

Hebrews 9:9 (AMP)

I love structure and knowing what's expected of me. When I'm feeling particularly anxious or overwhelmed, I create a new to-do list to bring order to my world and calm my frazzled nerves. I don't think I'm alone. A huge industry of time management experts exists to offer us ways to organize our lives into bite-sized, manageable tasks.

The satisfaction of scratching to-dos off a list can extend to religion as well. I'm convinced that humans are a religious bunch, even when they claim to be atheists or "non-religious." The "religious" go to church, give money, feed the poor. The "non-religious" care for the environment or join social causes as their acts of worship. Both groups search for a way to feel good, to clear the conscience. People everywhere—young or old, rich or poor, religious or not—are simply seeking peace for their souls.

But peace is elusive. The salvation we seek isn't found by following all the rules or checking a box. Even when we think we've got the rules covered, we find one more rule we can't satisfy or one more task we just can't complete. The answer isn't following rules; the solution is faith. Sinners have always been saved by faith—even in the Old Testament when God's list of requirements was long and complicated. The rules represented religion, but following those rules was impossible.

Going to church, feeding the poor, and caring for the environment are admirable activities. But dos and don'ts can never clear the conscience. God tells us that regulations were designed to show people their need of a savior. Following the rules doesn't please God. Only faith pleases God.

Read Today's Scripture:
Hebrews 9:1-10 and Hosea 6:6

1. Based on Hebrews 9:10, what are some examples of external regulations that exist in our religious practices today?

   _____

   _____

   _____

   _____

2. What does Hosea 6:6 say about what God desires from us?

   _____

   _____

   _____

   _____

Today's Journal:

In what ways are you trying to please God by following rules? How can you move from following rules to living by faith?

Day 2. Without the Shedding of Blood

Indeed, under the law almost everything is purified with blood, and without the shedding of blood there is no forgiveness of sins.

Hebrew 9:22

The newspaper reported that Nayati Moodliar was last seen wearing green shorts and a white t-shirt. The twelve-year-old boy was grabbed by two men on his way to school that spring morning in Kuala Lampur.[20]

Moments after the kidnapping, the ransom demand arrived. The family tried everything—urgent pleas online and on the local news. The Prime Minister even took to Twitter to beg for the boy's safety. The thought of a scared child stirred the community to action, and thousands of people across the globe came together on Facebook to support the family as they searched for the child. But nothing worked. All efforts were met with silence.

In the end, despite negotiation attempts by the authorities and in the face of great debate about giving in to kidnappers' demands, the family paid the ransom. How could they not? And to the great relief of his family and friends, Nayati Moodliar was returned home safely after one week of captivity.

Just as Nayati was held by his kidnappers, we are held hostage by our sin. Before I understood the true price of my freedom, I had a nagging sense inside of me that I needed to pay something to balance the scales somehow—an extra good deed or one more kind word. When I knew I was wrong, I often tried to correct my error by doing something right.

But freedom comes at great price. In God's eyes, the price for forgiveness is steep. No amount of payback can truly fix our wrongs. For the Jews, the price involved the blood of animals as payment for the sins people committed. But the payment was strictly temporary. The sacrifice had to be repeated. The only sacrifice powerful enough to have a lasting impact is the blood of Jesus. His is the only sacrifice that truly balances the scales. His blood is the last blood that needs to be shed in payment for sin.

God's Word tells us, "the wages of sin is death" (Romans 6:23). In other words, the price is blood. A ransom must be paid. Will you accept that the blood of Jesus is the ransom paid for your sin?

Read Today's Scripture:
Hebrews 9:11-22 and Luke 22:20

1. Based on Hebrews 9:11-22, how does the blood of Jesus compare with the blood of the animals used in Jewish sacrifice?

   _____

   _____

   _____

   _____

2. How does the blood of Christ cleanse our consciences (v. 14)? What does this mean to you personally? Are you willing to let the blood of Christ cleanse your conscience or are you still insisting on using your own actions to try to cleanse yourself?

   _____

   _____

   _____

   _____

Today's Journal:

Do you suffer from a conscience that has not been cleansed? If so, pause and thank Jesus for His sacrifice on your behalf. Perhaps you can pray Hebrews 9:15 and thank Jesus for being the ransom that set you free from your sins.

Day 3. Once for All

But as it is, he has appeared once for all at the end of the ages to put away sin by the sacrifice of himself.

Hebrews 9:26b

Have you ever heard a school-aged kid say, "When am I ever going to use math anyway?" Well, today is the day.

Mathematically, we prove something to be true if it meets criteria that are both necessary and sufficient. Let's use the example of a square. To be a square, an object must have four sides. But while it's necessary to have four sides, it's not sufficient because a rectangle also has four sides. On the other hand, some conditions are sufficient but not always necessary. For instance, in school, a student who earns an A is guaranteed to pass the course. In other words, an A is a sufficient condition for passing the course, but it isn't necessary because students who earn a B or a C will also pass the course.

To prove something to be true, like the square, we sometimes need a multitude of necessary conditions that together become sufficient. That is, they all must exist at once for the answer to be true. In our example, a square must have four sides, all straight, all equal length, joined at the ends, lying in a plane, with four 90 degree angles, etc. If we meet all these criteria, then, and only then, are we guaranteed a square.

Necessary and sufficient.

The Levitical sacrifices were not sufficient, but they were necessary because God required them. Under the Mosaic Law, a different type of sacrifice was brought for each sin, and each time a sin was committed, a new sacrifice had to be offered. Many conditions, but none providing permanent salvation. All necessary, but not sufficient. Jesus offered one single sacrifice for all our many sins.

Some people treat Christ as necessary, but not sufficient. That is, they believe in "Christ plus…" For them, the requirement may be

Christ plus baptism. Christ plus joining a church. Or Christ plus ritual. Others see Christ as sufficient, but not necessary. They may believe that Christianity is fine for you, but not for them. They seem to think that all attempts to gain forgiveness are equally acceptable.

As we saw yesterday, blood must be shed. Someone always had to die—the *necessary* condition. Thank God that Jesus' blood is absolutely *sufficient*. Having met all the criteria, Jesus' sacrifice—once for all—guarantees our salvation.

Read Today's Scripture:
Hebrews 9:23-28 and Romans 8:35-39

1. How does understanding Jesus' sacrifice in Hebrews 9:23-28 impact your life as a believer?

   _____

   _____

   _____

   _____

2. What does Romans 8:35 say about the sufficiency of Christ?

   _____

   _____

   _____

   _____

Today's Journal:

What is your response to God's Word today as you strengthen your faith? Which is more difficult for you to accept—that Jesus' sacrifice was necessary or that it is sufficient?

Day 4. The Superior Sacrifice

But in these sacrifices there is a reminder of sins every year. For it is impossible for the blood of bulls and goats to take away sins.

Hebrews 10:3-4

The Hunger Games by Suzanne Collins is the immensely popular tale of a world gone wrong. In this dystopian novel, the United States is ruled by a cruel totalitarian government. The Capital continually reminds its citizens of their prior rebellion by insisting that each district send one girl and one boy each year to fight to the death in gladiator-style games called the Hunger Games. The story is fast-paced and gripping. But its premise is all wrong.

In the world Collins creates, the sacrifices never end. The reminders continue year after year. No hope is ever offered. No redemption exists. Suzanne Collins paints a distorted and sad picture of a world where the same ugliness continues, no matter who is in charge.

Unlike the citizens of the thirteen districts ruled by the Capital in *The Hunger Games*, we have hope. In Jesus Christ, the sacrifices are finished. Though the Jewish sacrificial system was an annual reminder of sin, Jesus' sacrifice brought the old system to an end. His sacrifice took away sin, something that nothing else could accomplish. That's why John the Baptist could proclaim, "Behold! The Lamb of God who takes away the sin of the world!" (John 1:29)

That is good news. We don't have to look forward to the bleak world presented in popular young adult fiction. Our future is bright. Our story has a happy ending.

Read Today's Scripture:
Hebrews 10:1-7 and Psalm 40:6-8

1. According to Hebrews 10:1-7, what is the limitation in the old sacrificial system?

2. Based on Psalm 40:6-8, what does God think about sacrifices and offerings?

Today's Journal:
God guarantees that your story will have a happy ending. How does that help you develop a faith that endures?

Day 5. Made Perfect

For by a single offering he has perfected for all time those who are being sanctified.

Hebrews 10:14

A crushing dark weight. That's what condemnation feels like to me. It's the ugly sensation that makes me want to withdraw from God and from others. Every time I remember an old sin, guilt and condemnation threaten to overwhelm me yet again.

Conviction is entirely different. For me, that's the realization that something I've said, done, or thought doesn't line up with what God desires for me. Conviction is eye-opening; condemnation makes me want to squeeze my eyes shut. Conviction motivates me to change. Condemnation makes me cringe and hide.

Today's study contains two important truths. First, God doesn't take sin lightly. He condemns it, in fact. Romans 8:3-4 says, "He condemned sin in the flesh, in order that the righteous requirement of the law might be fulfilled in us..." I'm right to agree with God that my sin should be condemned. The second truth is that though God condemns sin, He doesn't condemn me. Romans 8:1 states, "There is therefore now no condemnation for those who are in Christ Jesus."

Hebrews 10:14 is the cure for our condemnation. When we accept Christ as our personal savior, we are "perfected." The Greek word is *telioo*, which means "to complete," which literally means "to accomplish."[21] However, as Christians, we're still "being sanctified." The Greek word is *hagiazo*, meaning "to be set apart for God, to sanctify, to make a person the opposite of *koinos* (common)."[22] This verse reminds us that we'll continue to struggle with sin while God cleans us up for a holy purpose. The road to holiness is bumpy, but we don't need to wallow in condemnation along the way.

**Read Today's Scripture:
Hebrews 10:8-18 and Romans 8:1-3**

1. In the NIV, Hebrews 10:14 reads, "Because by one sacrifice he has made perfect forever those who are being made holy." What does the difference between "has made perfect" and "are being made holy" imply to you?

   _____
   _____
   _____
   _____

2. As you grow as a believer, in what ways are you being made holy?

   _____
   _____
   _____
   _____

3. Do you ever struggle with condemnation? How can you apply Romans 8:1-3 in those circumstances?

   _____
   _____
   _____
   _____

Today's Journal:

How do you respond to what the Lord has shown you today? Perhaps you can use this opportunity to ask the Lord to convict you of any hidden sin in your life so that you can confess it to Him and be free. And then thank Him for the freedom from condemnation He has provided.

Final Thoughts

When we signed the mortgage on our house, we signed a document that gave the true ownership of our home to the bank. They now hold the title, and we own a slip of paper that says how much money we owe. Month after month, we send the bank our mortgage payment, but the loan hasn't been fully satisfied yet. It won't be for many years. Someday, though, we hope to finish paying for the house and on that day, we'll receive the title. On that day, the loan will be redeemed—paid in full.

The payment for our sin doesn't just disappear when we repent. The punishment is still handed down, but it is handed down to Jesus instead of to us. We can be healed because He died. We can live godly lives because Christ's death on the cross sets us free from the cell in which we were imprisoned. Jesus is the superior and final sacrifice. His final payment satisfied the wrath of God and freed us from the penalty of sin. Seeing the reality of what Christ accomplished on the cross gives us the power to cultivate a faith that endures.

Week 6.
Jesus Credits Faith As Righteousness

C. S. Lewis calls it *undeception*. "A startling experience of awareness—moments when deception is uncovered and the cause is seen clearly from within. Moments when blind spots are replaced with reality."[23]

Isaiah and Peter both experienced undeception. The year that his earthly king died, Isaiah saw the King of Kings on the throne.

> "Holy, holy, holy is the Lord of hosts; the whole earth is full of his glory!" And the foundations of the thresholds shook at the voice of him who called, and the house was filled with smoke. And I said: "Woe is me! For I am lost; for I am a man of unclean lips, and I dwell in the midst of a people of unclean lips; for my eyes have seen the King, the Lord of hosts!" (Isaiah 6:3b-5)

Peter experienced the same undeception. Despite an unsuccessful night of fishing, he obeyed Jesus' request to fish some more.

> But when Simon Peter saw it, he fell down at Jesus' knees, saying, "Depart from me, for I am a sinful man, O Lord." For he and all who were with him were astonished at the catch of fish that they had taken. (Luke 5:8-9)

Both men caught a glimpse of the holy. Both men fell to the ground at the sight of their own unholiness. Undeception.

God allowed them to see their unholiness, but He didn't leave them wallowing in their shame. He came to the rescue. The seraph touched Isaiah's lips with a coal from the altar and his sin was taken away (Isaiah 6:6-7). Jesus told Peter, "Do not be afraid; from now on you will be catching men" (Luke 5:10). Both men heard God's call. Both followed.

I'm grateful God doesn't leave me wallowing in my shame either—aware of my sinfulness but helpless to remedy it. When I see my own condition, I want to hide from God and cry, "Depart from me." Then I remember that I've been saved by grace (Ephesians 2:8-10). Though I have no righteousness of my own, God sees faith and credits it as righteousness. He did that for the generations described in Hebrews, and He does the same for us today.

The people mentioned in Hebrews chapter 11—the hall of fame of faith—are not listed because they did mighty deeds (though some did). They are listed because their faith pleased God.

Day 1. Therefore, Let Us…

Therefore, brothers, since we have confidence to enter the holy places by the blood of Jesus…

Hebrews 10:19

Fixing someone dinner, volunteering at church, and doing a good job at work are all admirable things to do. But I have to ask myself, why am I doing them?

"My friend will appreciate me. *Therefore* let me take her a hot meal."

"My boss will reward me. *Therefore* let me do a good job."

Therefore signals cause and effect. I recognize that many counterfeit causes motivate me. Praise feels good. Right actions, wrong motivation. Even if I do the right thing, God will test me one day to reveal what caused me to perform good deeds.

> But each one should be careful how he builds. For no one can lay any foundation other than the one already laid, which is Jesus Christ. If any man builds on this foundation using gold, silver, costly stones, wood, hay or straw, his work will be shown for what it is, because the Day will bring it to light. It will be revealed with fire, and the fire will test the quality of each man's work. (1 Corinthians 3:10-13 NIV)

What should drive me to act like a Christian? Not the appreciation of my friends or the reward at work. Instead, the real motivator is Jesus Christ. He is the only sure foundation, that is, the only worthy cause. Some of our works—the gold, silver, costly stones—will stand the test. But work that is motivated by anything less than our devotion to Jesus Christ will not endure.

"Therefore, brothers, since we have confidence to enter the holy places by the blood of Jesus…let us…" (Hebrews 10:19ff). The invitation in Hebrews is "let us" do the right thing for the right reason: the blood of Jesus.

Read Today's Scripture:
Hebrews 10:19-25 and 1 John 3:11-24

1. In Hebrews 10:19-25, what are the five exhortations (things written to motivate us to do something) that follow the words "let us"?

   _____

   _____

   _____

   _____

2. Based on 1 John 3:11-24, why are we to love one another? How do we demonstrate that love to one another?

   _____

   _____

   _____

   _____

Today's Journal:

Do you ever find your heart condemning you as described in 1 John 3:19? What is your response to God's encouragement that you can set your heart at rest in His presence today?

Day 2. The Call To Persevere

For if we go on sinning deliberately after receiving the knowledge of the truth, there no longer remains a sacrifice for sins.

Hebrews 10:26

A graduating senior gave advice to the younger students after class. "You can pass this class one of two ways: Learn how to do the homework so that you can answer the questions correctly on the test, or master the material. The second way is more satisfying." Wise beyond his years, that student figured out the difference between knowing facts and the deep understanding that comes with mastery of the subject matter.

The Greek language has several words for "know." Some folks know (Greek word *ginosko*) who God is. They have a practical knowledge of God and of God's requirements. In other words, they know what to do to answer homework questions correctly. Others have a "full, personal, precise, and correct" knowledge (Greek word *epiginosko*). That is, they know God or God's requirements in a "personal, conscious way."[24]

> For although they knew [*ginosko*] God, they did not honor him as God or give thanks to him… (Romans 1:21)
> And since they did not see fit to acknowledge [*epignosis*] God, God gave them up to a debased mind to do what ought not to be done… Though they know [*epiginosko*] God's righteous decree that those who practice such things deserve to die, they not only do them but give approval to those who practice them. (Romans 1:28, 32)

Our passage in Hebrews today opens with those who have personal, conscious *epignosis* of God's decree but who reject His grace in spite of that knowledge. Where else can they find hope? Nowhere. Salvation is found in no one else. If we go on sinning in spite of what we know, we're guilty of trampling Jesus underfoot (Hebrews 10:29). That's serious. Instead, we want to be among those who develop a faith that endures. We want to be among "those who have faith and preserve their souls" (Hebrews 10:39).

Read Today's Scripture:
Hebrews 10:26-39, Romans 2:4, and Psalm 1

1. What does the author of Hebrews mean in verse 26 when he writes, "go on sinning deliberately"? According to Romans 2:4, how can people "presume" on the Lord (the NIV translates this "show contempt")?

   _____

   _____

   _____

   _____

2. What are some of the characteristics of the man who is "blessed" in Psalm 1? How does he prevent himself from sinning?

   _____

   _____

   _____

   _____

Today's Journal:

How do you respond to Psalm 1:1-2 today? In what areas of your life are you struggling to persevere? What has God shown you in His Word today about faith that endures?

Day 3. By Faith We Understand

Now faith is the assurance of things hoped for, the conviction of things not seen.

Hebrews 11:1

While traveling in China one year, we enjoyed the beauty of Huangshan (Yellow Mountain). After a spectacular cable car ride, we hiked to a hotel so we could spend the night at the mountaintop. The view reminded me of the jagged mountain peaks depicted in many Chinese watercolors.

During the trip, our guide described how the stones had been pitted when the water of glaciers receded millions of years ago.

To me, it seemed that the pitted stones were more likely the result of the great flood described in Genesis. But to many university professors, believing the "creation myth" seems crazy. They might ask, "What about all the scientific evidence?"

My answer is simple. I believe what God says in the Bible. I don't have to see in order to believe. Had I lived hundreds of years ago, all physical evidence at the time would have suggested that the earth was flat. And yet God's Word said that the earth was round: "It is he who sits above the circle of the earth" (Isaiah 40:22). I would have had a choice—do I believe the evidence before my eyes that tells me the horizon is flat, or do I believe God's Word that tells me the earth is round? I choose God's Word. Today, "evidence" suggests that the earth is millions of years old. Yet God's Word tells us that He accomplished creation by His very word, and He didn't need matter in order to create more matter. In other words, "What is seen was not made out of things that are visible" (Hebrews 11:3).

Hebrews 11:1 tells us that "faith is the assurance of things hoped for." The Greek word for "assurance" is *hypostasis* and can be translated "substance, what really exists under any appearance, reality, essential nature." The same word is used in Hebrews 1:3, which affirms that Jesus is the exact representation (the *hypostasis* or essence) of God's being. Our faith has substance and is based on real evidence. You and I are not standing on shaky ground. We stand on a firm foundation.

Read Today's Scripture:
Hebrews 11:1-3 and Romans 1:20-23

1. Based on Romans 1:20-23, what does creation tell us about God?

   _____

   _____

   _____

   _____

2. Can you describe how your faith has made you certain of what you do not see (Hebrews 11:1)?

   _____

   _____

   _____

   _____

Today's Journal:

What is your response to God's Word today about faith that endures? Is your faith on a firm foundation or are you standing on shaky ground?

Day 4. Commended by God

And without faith it is impossible to please him, for whoever would draw near to God must believe that he exists and that he rewards those who seek him.

Hebrews 11:6

Today we begin our journey into the "hall of fame of faith" as some have called this chapter of Hebrews. We glimpse God's perspective by looking at the lives of three men: Abel, Enoch, and Noah. These men and all the others in the hall of fame have their flaws. Yet, God looks at them through the lens of faith and records them as faithful servants.

This passage reminds us that God focuses on faith rather than works. These people aren't necessarily being commended for what they did. They were far from perfect. They are commended because their faith motivated them to do what they did. "Without faith, it is impossible to please God."

The Old Testament describes Enoch's life as a man of God (Genesis 5:22-24), and Noah is listed as a man who "walked with God" (Genesis 6:9). Both of them showed evidence of great faith (see Jude 14), but the Bible doesn't provide much information about Abel's faith. All we know is that his sacrifice was looked on with favor by God (Genesis 4:3-5). Though we don't learn the details of Abel's faith in Genesis, we learn in Hebrews that he demonstrated faith when he offered the better sacrifice.

Abel and Noah died. Enoch never died. And yet all three men have a lasting testimony of faith. These men pleased God and were commended for their faith.

Read Today's Scripture:
Hebrews 11:4-7 and Genesis 5:22-24

1. What did Abel, Enoch, and Noah do that prompted God to mention them in the hall of fame of faith?

   _____

   _____

   _____

   _____

2. What does "Enoch walked with God" mean? Can you think of any people in your life that can be described like this? Can you be described as one who walks with God?

   _____

   _____

   _____

   _____

Today's Journal:

How do you respond to what God is showing you today about faith that endures? If God were going to write a sentence about your faith, what specific act would He mention?

Day 5. By Faith Abraham

By faith Sarah herself received power to conceive, even when she was past the age, since she considered him faithful who had promised.

Hebrews 11:11

Many children see the glass half-full rather than half-empty. If mom promises ice cream, then they count the ice cream as a done deal. If they hear, "Just wait until your daddy gets home!" then they know that dire circumstances lie ahead. As they grow older and the authorities in their lives disappoint them, oftentimes their glass half-full approach changes. They become less certain of what lies ahead when the one who promised fails to deliver.

Abraham and Sarah, despite their many shortcomings, counted Him who promised as faithful. Abraham is noted for his obedience and willingness to live like a stranger "in a foreign land" (Hebrews 11:9). Why such a glass half-full approach on their part? They were "[waiting expectantly and confidently] looking forward to the city which has fixed and firm foundations, whose Architect and Builder is God" (Hebrews 11:10 AMP). Abraham knew God. He knew that the One who made the promise would keep the promise. God defines faith in Hebrews 11:1 as "being sure of what we hope for and certain of what we do not see" (NIV). Sarah also demonstrated that kind of faith when "she judged him faithful who had promised" (Hebrews 11:11 KJV).

Read Today's Scripture:
Hebrews 11:8-19 and Romans 4:18-24

1. Based on Romans 4:18-24, why might Abraham have given up hope that what God promised would ever come to pass? How did Abraham actually respond to his circumstances? What was God's response?

   _____

   _____

   _____

   _____

2. Based on Hebrews 11:13-16, what should our day-to-day perspective be? How can we demonstrate the kind of faith that these men and women were commended for?

   _____

   _____

   _____

   _____

Today's Journal:

Has the Holy Spirit shown you where you might not be demonstrating the kind of faith that pleases God? Maybe you can pray with the man in Mark 9:24—"Lord, I believe; help thou my unbelief" (KJV). Lord, cultivate in me a faith that endures.

Final Thoughts

Jesus pleased God. After Jesus was baptized, the Scriptures say, "And [God's] voice came from heaven, 'You are my beloved Son; with you I am well pleased'" (Mark 1:11). If God is more than a kind old grandfather who pats children on their heads and gives them peppermints, then what does it take to please God?

I know that faith pleases God, and yet I find it easy to slip into believing that somehow my actions are more important. Maybe I have to join the choir, teach a Sunday school class, or feed the homeless. Perhaps I need to carefully tiptoe through the Ten Commandments: avoid idolatry, honor my parents, and keep the Sabbath. Maybe then I can please God.

All these things are good, but they are effects, not causes. Only one thing will actually please God. Trusting Him. That's it. One day I'm going to stand before God, and I won't be able to point to my Christian résumé. Instead, He'll look past all that—just as He did with Abel, Enoch, Noah, and Abraham—and inspect my faith. He'll be looking for the kind of faith they had: faith that trusted in the One who made the promise more than in the present circumstances.

Week 7.

Faith Is Followed by Inheritance

I was still working full time when I became pregnant with our second child. Our firstborn was only six months old, and we were worn out trying to juggle babysitting with our work schedules. My husband and I agreed that when the second baby came, I would resign and stay home full time. What a relief.

I worked the next eight months knowing the joy that was waiting for me. I was soon going home. My perspective at work changed. My daily stress faded. Though my day-to-day work hadn't changed, a burden had been lifted from me.

In our study this week, we'll see pictures of those who turned their eyes toward what was promised rather than fixing their sights on their present circumstances. By faith, Moses chose the persecuted life of his people rather than the privileged life of royalty. By faith, Rahab trusted the God of the Hebrews rather than the strength of her people. By faith Gideon, Barak, Samson… This great cloud of witnesses looked ahead to the inheritance that belonged to the people of God.

These men and women desired "a better country, that is, a heavenly one. Therefore God is not ashamed to be called their God, for he has prepared for them a city" (Hebrews 11:16). We are citizens of this better country as well. We are strangers and aliens here; our inheritance is in heaven. The anticipation I remember from those months before our son was born is only a taste of the hope we can experience as we look ahead to the city God has prepared.

Day 1. By Faith Moses

He considered the reproach of Christ greater wealth than the treasures of Egypt, for he was looking to the reward.

Hebrews 11:26

A glimpse of God changed Moses forever. It gave Moses the courage to lead the Israelites through the Red Sea, and it gave him the desire to pray for them in spite of their complaints. A glimpse of God changed Moses from a fearful runaway into a friend of God. Though his first encounter came at the burning bush, perhaps his most touching encounter was in Exodus 33:12-34:8 where God showed Moses His glory while He hid Moses in the cleft of the rock:

> "But," he said, "you cannot see my face, for man shall not see me and live." And the Lord said, "Behold, there is a place by me where you shall stand on the rock, and while my glory passes by I will put you in a cleft of the rock, and I will cover you with my hand until I have passed by." (Exodus 33:20-22)

Jesus is the image of our invisible God (Colossians 1:15). No one can see God and live, so God made Himself visible in the form of Jesus Christ. He came to earth clothed in flesh; the invisible became visible. "And the Word became flesh and dwelt among us, and we have seen his glory, glory as of the only Son from the Father, full of grace and truth" (John 1:14). Many people saw Jesus while He was here on earth, but not all really perceived who He was—God Himself.

We too can "see" the invisible God. We're invited to "seek the Lord while he may be found" (Isaiah 55:6). We're invited into a relationship with Jesus, to be changed forever. Like Moses, we can persevere because we see the One who is invisible. "So we fix our eyes not on what is seen, but on what is unseen. For what is seen is temporary, but what is unseen is eternal" (2 Corinthians 4:18 NIV). This is the faith in Hebrews 11:1—we are "sure of what we hope for and certain of what we do not see" (NIV).

Read Today's Scripture:
Hebrews 11:20-28 and Exodus 33:12-23

1. What did the people in Hebrews 11 do by faith? Why did Moses demonstrate such courage?

   _____

   _____

   _____

   _____

2. In what ways can we glimpse the One who is "invisible"? Can you describe the last time you had such an experience?

   _____

   _____

   _____

   _____

Today's Journal:

Have you gained any fresh insight from the passages in Hebrews or Exodus that you can share? How can seeing "the One who is invisible" strengthen your faith?

Day 2. Divine Approval

> *His master said to him, "Well done, good and faithful servant. You have been faithful over a little; I will set you over much. Enter into the joy of your master."*
>
> Matthew 25:23

If God were to pen your story, would He "commend" your faith (Hebrews 11:39 NIV)? Would your faith be met with "divine approval" (AMP)?

On my best day, I don't obey God completely. Even when I think I get it right, I probably don't. Thank God He looks at us through the filter of faith. Joshua 2 records an example of faith in spite of imperfect behavior. Rahab lied to the king when she helped the Hebrew spies escape. Does that mean God needed her to lie or that He even approved of her lies? I've probably been in situations where I've done the wrong thing for the right reason. But I don't believe God compromises; neither is He looking for me to "help" Him accomplish His will. Instead of blessing her *because* she lied, He looked at her heart and blessed her *in spite of* the lie. Thank God that He looks at the heart, and He credits faith as righteousness.

Barak is another unlikely character that receives divine approval. When Deborah told him to lead the army into battle, he responds, "If you will go with me, I will go, but if you will not go with me, I will not go" (Judges 4:8). Hardly a shining example of faith. Yet Barak is listed among some very distinguished company. In fact, Hebrews 11:32 tells us that Barak won "divine approval."

God looks past our works. Our faith will be tested as we face persecution and trials. God expects us to demonstrate faith, and in the end, we want to hear Him say, "Well done, good and faithful servant..." (Matthew 25:23).

Read Today's Scripture:
Hebrews 11:29-40, Matthew 5:10-12, and Daniel 3:16-18

1. In Hebrews 11:29-40, what are a few of the actions that were performed by faith?

   _____

   _____

   _____

   _____

2. Based on Matthew 5:10-12, what are some trials we'll face in which we'll have the opportunity to demonstrate faith? How did Shadrach, Meshach, and Abednego demonstrate faith in Daniel 3:16-18?

   _____

   _____

   _____

   _____

Today's Journal:

Briefly describe the last time your faith was tested. Is there any area of your life where the Lord is calling you to act by faith today?

Day 3. Those Things That Hinder

Therefore, since we are surrounded by so great a cloud of witnesses, let us also lay aside every weight, and sin which clings so closely, and let us run with endurance the race that is set before us, looking to Jesus, the founder and perfecter of our faith, who for the joy that was set before him endured the cross, despising the shame, and is seated at the right hand of the throne of God.

Hebrews 12:1-2

I've learned from experience what to pack for a trip and what to leave behind. Here are a couple of my favorite packing secrets: First, I limit the shoes. They're bulky and take up valuable space, so I like to wear the same pair for the entire trip if possible. I also reduce the number of pieces of heavy clothing like blue jeans and sweaters. One sweater is usually enough for a week. I've learned that dragging a giant suitcase up and down stairs, in and out of trains hurts my back, makes me anxious, and generally prevents me from enjoying my trip. Even worse, I have no space to carry home souvenirs because I'm already loaded down with stuff from home.

In my personal life, I have "baggage" that weighs me down. Some are innocent distractions like hobbies, books, or movies. Some are less innocent—sins that entangle me and drag me away from God's purpose. In all cases, they pull my attention away from God's agenda and draw me toward my own.

I don't want to carry an analogy too far, but we can see that being distracted by a spiritual "overfilled suitcase" can slow us down. The weight is distracting, exhausting, stressful, and prevents us from completing the task before us. Hebrews 12:1 encourages us to "lay aside every weight, and sin which clings so closely, and let us run with endurance the race that is set before us." Let's quit burdening ourselves with the many distractions and fix our eyes instead on Jesus, the One who initiated the race and the only one who can enable us to finish it successfully.

Read Today's Scripture:
Hebrews 12:1-3, Romans 5:3-5, and Luke 10:40-42

1. What are the weights that seem to hinder Martha in Luke 10:40-42?

   _____

   _____

   _____

   _____

2. Can you identify any of the weights or sins in your own life that are hindering your ability to "run the race" described in Hebrews 12:1-3?

   _____

   _____

   _____

   _____

3. Based on Romans 5:3-5, what does perseverance produce in our lives?

   _____

   _____

   _____

   _____

Today's Journal:

How can you fix your eyes on Jesus so that you will not grow weary and lose heart (Hebrews 12:3)? Are there any specific Bible verses that strengthen your faith?

Day 4. The Encouragement of Discipline

> *For the moment all discipline seems painful rather than pleasant, but later it yields the peaceful fruit of righteousness to those who have been trained by it.*
>
> Hebrews 12:11

The Lord disciplined me one night when I refused to get out of bed.

It all started when my children were babies, and I had a hard time finding a few quiet minutes during the day to spend with my Bible. Sometimes I got up at 3:00 a.m. to feed a baby and then, once the child was quiet again, I was wide-awake. So I started using the time to study God's Word. After the kids began sleeping through the night, I was often so busy during the day that I asked the Lord to continue waking me up when all else was quiet so that He could have my undivided attention.

One night, I sensed the Lord waking me up at 3:00 a.m., but I was tired and didn't want to respond. I felt the nudge more than once, but I ignored it and rolled over. I negotiated with God. I had nothing scheduled for the next morning. I'd have plenty of time to read my Bible and pray then, so why did I have to get out of bed in the middle of the night? Satisfied with my own logic, I went back to sleep.

When morning came, I settled into my favorite spot with my Bible and a fresh cup of coffee to enjoy some quiet time. Immediately, I felt the "rod of discipline." The reminder of the wake-up call from the night before came flooding to my mind. I knew that I had disobeyed a direct order and that I was experiencing the Father's discipline.

No discipline is fun, but all discipline should be encouraging. I don't enjoy having my errors brought to my attention. When it happens, however, I realize that I belong to One who is wise enough to see the road ahead and will actively discipline me for my own good. God's discipline is proof that I'm a Christian. I can be sure that I'm saved when God treats me as His child (Hebrews 12:7). And that is very good news indeed.

Read Today's Scripture:
Hebrews 12:4-11 and 1 Chronicles 21:8-13

1. Based on Hebrews 12:4-11, what does it mean to be subject to the Father as He disciplines us? Can you think of any ways that the Father has disciplined you?

   _____

   _____

   _____

   _____

2. How was David disciplined in 1 Chronicles 21:8-13? Why did he choose the third option?

   _____

   _____

   _____

   _____

Today's Journal:

Be courageous today. Ask the Lord to discipline you—to show you where you are not living according to His will. Ask Him to work in you—"to will and to work for his good pleasure" (Philippians 2:13). Ask Him to show you how to develop a faith that endures.

Day 5. Citizens in Heaven

But rather, you have come to Mount Zion, even to the city of the living God, the heavenly Jerusalem, and to countless multitudes of angels in festal gathering, And to the church (assembly) of the Firstborn who are registered [as citizens] in heaven, and to the God Who is Judge of all, and to the spirits of the righteous (the redeemed in heaven) who have been made perfect.

Hebrews 12:22-23 (AMP)

On a flight home one year, I found myself seated next to a family that was immigrating to the USA from the Middle East. Delighted to discover that I spoke Arabic, they immediately clung to me as their link between the life they were leaving and the unknown that lay ahead. They overflowed with nervous chatter about the choices they would face as citizens of one country but residents of another. What foods would they eat? What schools would the kids attend? Who would their neighbors be? They had heard of other immigrants whose children had abandoned the old way of life. They probably didn't realize that they too would soon struggle to preserve their culture in a new country with its unfamiliar traditions, foods, and language.

As Christians, we live in a country that's not our own. We're not comfortable with its foreign diet and strange-sounding language. We are strangers and aliens. Despite all the pressure to blend in, we know that our citizenship is in heaven—it is our permanent home. We haven't immigrated for good. We're headed to our eternal home. God's Word describes us as the "church (assembly) of the Firstborn who are registered [as citizens] in heaven" (Hebrews 12:23 AMP). May our daily lives reflect that truth.

Read Today's Scripture:
Hebrews 12:12-24 and Psalm 84:7

1. What are some of the warnings found in Hebrews 12:12-24?

   _____

   _____

   _____

   _____

2. What will the city of God, Zion, be like according to Psalm 84:7 and Hebrews 12:22-24?

   _____

   _____

   _____

   _____

Today's Journal:

How do you respond to God's warnings and encouragement today? In what ways do you find God calling you to demonstrate that your citizenship is in heaven, not on earth?

Final Thoughts

> *The pilgrims to the heavenly city may have to pass through many a valley of weeping, and many a thirsty desert; but wells of salvation shall be opened for them, and consolations sent for their support. Those that press forward in their Christian course, shall find God add grace to their graces. And those who grow in grace, shall be perfect in glory.*
>
> ~ Matthew Henry's Concise Commentary of the Bible[25]

I had been forced to take several trips back to back, and I was tired. I was only gone for a week, but I missed my husband and our children. I felt sorry for myself as I ate airport food, surrounded by germs. Loud cell phone conversations, stressed-out travelers, and harried flight attendants left me feeling harried and stressed out myself. I wanted to go home.

The anxiety upset my stomach, and soon all I could eat was crackers and chicken noodle soup from hotel room service. In just two more days, I could rest, but those two days couldn't go by fast enough. The sight of my husband and kids when they met me at the airport lifted my heart. I was home. I could rest.

The rest I experienced when I came home is just a taste of the rest we are offered in Christ. "He who dwells in the shelter of the Most High will abide in the shadow of the Almighty" (Psalm 91:1). This is home.

> My faith has found a resting place,
> Not in device or creed;
> I trust the ever-living One,
> His wounds for me shall plead.
>
> I need no other argument,
> I need no other plea,
> It is enough that Jesus died,
> And that He died for me.[26]

Week 8.
Jesus Equips Us To Do His Will

Satan gets a lot of credit. Everything from the flu to lost luggage is blamed on the enemy. I can't count the number of times I've heard Christian friends say, "Satan would love nothing more than _____." Just fill in the blank. Satan wants me to fight with my husband. Satan would love for me to mess up at work. Satan longs to see me fail. He's out to trick me, mislead me, destroy me. "Be sober-minded; be watchful. Your adversary the devil prowls around like a roaring lion, seeking someone to devour" (1 Peter 5:8).

If Satan can so easily cause us to miss God's will, does that mean God makes it difficult for us to find His will? Can't we trust God to direct us properly? Author Steve McVey encourages us to give more credit to God's ability to lead us into His will than we give to Satan's ability to mislead us.[27] Yes, we do have an enemy who is actively seeking our destruction, but we have One on our side who is greater. "For the eyes of the Lord run to and fro throughout the whole earth, to give strong support to those whose heart is blameless toward him" (2 Chronicles 16:9).

Developing a faith that endures requires that we trust God to accomplish His will in our lives. God's will is not some mysterious moving target. We trust that He'll give us words to say what He wants us to say and skills to do what He wants us to do. God told Jeremiah, "But the Lord said to me, 'Do not say, 'I am too young.' You must go to everyone I send you to and say whatever I command you. Do not be afraid of them for I am with you and will rescue you,' declares the Lord" (Jeremiah 1:7-8 NIV). As McVey puts it, "Doing God's will isn't something for us to figure out, but rather is something He accomplishes as we depend on Him."[28] This is the life of faith we are called to live as Christians.

Day 1. The Kingdom That Cannot Be Shaken

This phrase, "Yet once more," indicates the removal of things that are shaken—that is, things that have been made—in order that the things that cannot be shaken may remain.

Hebrews 12:27

Planet earth is temporary. It's going to be destroyed, and all the environmentally friendly choices in the world won't save it. Revelation 21:1 says, "Then I saw a new heaven and a new earth, for the first heaven and the first earth had passed away, and the sea was no more." God is going to stir things up and replace the temporary with the eternal.

Temporary things compete for my attention. I'm easily obsessed with my to-do lists and my calendar. I have an agenda to follow, and my world spins out of orbit when something goes wrong. I want to be the mature Christian who sees each circumstance as another opportunity to watch Jesus at work. Step by step He's changing me, but I'm not quite there yet. I'm still too easily distracted by the temporary. In times of crisis, I'm more likely to beg the Lord to release me from my trouble than I am to ask Him to show me how to grow through the crisis. I have to be shaken free from my agenda so that I can patiently allow Him to shift my focus to His eternal agenda.

Today's passage in Hebrews reminds me that God is in the business of removing those things that can be shaken so that the unshakable will remain.

Read Today's Scripture:
Hebrews 12:25-29 and Psalm 46

1. Based on Hebrews 12:27 and Psalm 46, what are the things that can be shaken?

   _____

   _____

   _____

   _____

2. Can you identify any areas of your life that have been shaken or are currently being shaken? Do you have a testimony you can share about how the Lord has changed your focus?

   _____

   _____

   _____

   _____

Today's Journal:

Meditate on Psalm 46 today and write your response below. How does this passage strengthen your faith?

Day 2. Love Others

> *But someone will say, "You have faith and I have works." Show me your faith apart from your works, and I will show you my faith by my works.*
>
> James 2:18

In school, I discovered that my friends and I said or "believed" one thing, but we often did another. I worked on one class project with a group of my friends who really wanted to do a good job. They listed all the reasons the project was important and ended each class with promises to finish the next step. Meeting after meeting, each student volunteered for one task or another.

"I'll collect some news articles," one said.

Another chimed in, "I'll write the introduction and include the data."

Everything seemed like it would be completed on time, but at the final deadline, several members failed to produce what they had promised. Though everyone claimed the project was important, only a few actually followed through with action.

If you spend enough time with people, you'll discover that we're a fickle bunch. I'm guilty as charged. I've often said one thing and done another. For instance, I may claim that I believe all people are entitled to the same respect, but if I show favoritism, then I show that I don't believe my own words.

In our Christian lives, our actions reveal a lot about what we believe. If we claim to trust the Lord, then we can't worry about finances. If we believe that God is serious about sin, then we can't dabble in our pet sins. Likewise with faith. We see the faith of the heroes of old, and we may even claim to have faith ourselves, but the proof is in our actions.

What acts are "prompted by your faith" (2 Thessalonians 1:11 NIV)? Isn't it interesting that the acts listed in Hebrews 13 aren't amazing feats that cause others to marvel? We're not called to perform miraculous deeds to demonstrate our faith. Rather we're simply to behave as Christians, worthy of our calling. Primarily, we're to demonstrate love for one another—the best indicator of our faith.

Read Today's Scripture:
Hebrews 13:1-8, 2 Thessalonians 1:11-12, and Ephesians 4:1-3

1. Can you identify any areas of your life where your actions reveal your true beliefs, either positive or negative?

2. Based on Hebrews 13:1-8 and Ephesians 4:1-3, what are some of the acts that we are instructed to do?

Today's Journal:

Is God calling you to act differently to demonstrate your faith? How do you respond to His call today?

Day 3. Legalism: A Strange Teaching

Do not be carried about by different and varied and alien teachings; for it is good for the heart to be established and ennobled and strengthened by means of grace (God's favor and spiritual blessing) and not [to be devoted to] foods [rules of diet and ritualistic meals], which bring no [spiritual] benefit or profit to those who observe them.

Hebrews 13:9 (AMP)

I always thought that legalism—that is, man-made religious rules—was something that other churches were guilty of. I never considered that I can be carried away by such "alien teachings" myself. I didn't identify myself among the Christians who require a certain type of clothing, accept a certain type of Christian music, or insist on a certain translation of the Bible. I assumed I was free from legalism, but I was wrong.

My friend Renee described her experience with legalism when she first became a Christian:

> When I first was saved, what little I knew from other Christians made me think that I should filter my mind. That meant television, the bar areas of restaurants, R-rated movies. I knew the Bible said to filter your mind, but I didn't know where in the Bible exactly. While on a trip to Israel, I was talking with a leader in my church, and he and his wife were discussing a certain television show they watch. I was immediately alarmed because he was a leader, and I questioned his authority. "What does the Bible say about that?" I asked with sincerity. His wife spoke up and told me I was being legalistic. When I asked what that meant, she explained that I was imposing my

convictions on someone else. It opened my eyes to my judgmental thoughts, and I never forgot it.

I had started my Christian journey with a checklist of what real Christians do and don't do. If someone watched something, said something, or drank something, then I crossed them off the Christian list in my mind. I was really good at being everyone else's Holy Spirit. As I have grown, I see how much time I spent doing this in my thoughts, and I can see how many people I checked off my list. Most of the time I saw this only when I also did or said things I thought I would never do again. The Holy Spirit poked me in my heart, reminded me of those past thoughts and revealed to me my own sin.

I heard a podcast clip from Curtis Jones' *Drive Thru the Bible*, which helped me understand legalism. This is what I summarized from listening to it. Using pornography as an example, he said, "Let's say a person is tempted by pornography and his friends are aware of it. His friends say, "Okay, you must have one of us present if you are going to be on your computer." They then say that he should really have three of his friends present if he is going to be on his computer. Next they say, "You know what, it is probably best if you remove the computer from your house—better yet don't even tempt yourself by going into the computer department at Best Buy. In fact, don't go to any stores that have computers you can turn on." Pastor Jones explained that we keep drawing the lines in the sand on the rules of another person's temptations and convictions.

It is so easy to point the finger with just a little bit of knowledge of what the Bible says. I thought I knew everything, but as I learn more, I feel foolish for having such a legalistic attitude.

Yesterday's passage, which encouraged Christ-like behavior, is immediately followed by today's passage, which warns us against legalism. No one sets out to become legalistic. Most man-made rules sneak into the church because they make sense to some degree. But carried too far, a preference by one individual can quietly grow into a requirement for church membership.

Like Renee, we all have either been guilty of applying man-made rules to other people or experienced the judgment of others ourselves. Legalism shifts our focus away from God's grace. When we yield to it, we mislead a lost world by suggesting that salvation involves an impossible set of rules in addition to simple faith. And finally, legalism divides the church. When a rule becomes more important than Jesus, controversy and confusion infect a congregation.

Please don't misunderstand me. Calling legalism a strange teaching doesn't mean we can throw all self-control out the window. The Bible has plenty to say about how we handle ourselves, as we studied yesterday. But the main thing is Jesus, not the man-made rituals we follow.

Read Today's Scripture:
Hebrews 13:9-10 and 1 Timothy 4:1-7

1. According to 1 Timothy 4:1-7, what are some of the godless myths that appeared in Paul and Timothy's day? Can you think of any "strange teachings" that are prevalent today?

   _____

   _____

   _____

   _____

2. According to 1 Timothy 4:6-7, what are some ways that Christians can counter the effects of incorrect teaching?

   _____

   _____

   _____

   _____

Today's Journal:

Has the Holy Spirit shown you anything new today? Can you identify any areas of legalism in your life that interfere with your ability to develop a faith that endures?

_____

_____

_____

_____

_____

_____

_____

_____

_____

_____

Day 4. Outside the Camp

Therefore Jesus also suffered and died outside the [city's] gate in order that He might purify and consecrate the people through [the shedding of] His own blood and set them apart as holy [for God].

Hebrews 13:12 (AMP)

In the Old Testament, the region "outside the camp" represented both holiness and judgment. It served a holy purpose because the priest burned the remainder of the sin offering outside the camp after the blood was sprinkled at the altar (Leviticus 4:12). Moses pitched the Tent of Meeting outside the camp, and the Israelites were invited to inquire of the Lord there (Exodus 33:7). "Outside the camp" also served the role of judgment because it was the place where sinners were punished by stoning (Leviticus 24:23) and ceremonially unclean people were confined (Numbers 31:19).

Jesus went outside the camp to suffer the judgment of the sinner and has become "our righteousness, holiness, and redemption" (1 Corinthians 1:30 NIV). The holy purpose was fulfilled when He became the sin offering that was sacrificed in our place. The judgment was satisfied because "God made him who had no sin to be sin for us, so that in him we might become the righteousness of God" (2 Corinthians 5:21 NIV). Jesus was stricken and afflicted, and by His wounds we are healed (Isaiah 53:4-5).

Read Today's Scripture:
Hebrews 13:11-16 and Isaiah 53:3-8

1. What does Hebrews 13:13 mean when it says to "go to him outside the camp, bearing the disgrace he bore?" What motivates us to go to Jesus outside the camp?

2. According to Isaiah 53:3-8, in what ways was Jesus outside the camp for us?

Today's Journal:

How does your understanding of the disgrace that is "outside the camp" affect your outlook as you develop a faith that endures?

Day 5. Final Exhortations

> *Now may the God of peace who brought again from the dead our Lord Jesus, the great shepherd of the sheep, by the blood of the eternal covenant, equip you with everything good that you may do his will, working in us that which is pleasing in his sight, through Jesus Christ, to whom be glory forever and ever. Amen.*
>
> Hebrews 13:20-21

Teachers have tried all kinds of tricks to prompt kids to do what they want them to do. They've tried threats and bribes. Some have used competition to persuade kids to perform ("First one to turn in the homework earns the prize"), and others have used shame to prevent kids from doing poorly ("You don't want to be like Susie, do you?"). Some tricks work—briefly—and others not at all.

As parents, we know the difference between *making* a child do something and *motivating* the child to do it. A child who is motivated to go to church is more likely to continue in church once he or she is out of the house. The problem is, though, it's difficult to motivate anyone to do anything.

The end of Hebrews describes the only lasting motivation for living the Christian life. It starts with God doing a powerful work outside of us and ends with God working in us to do His will. First, God. He's the God of peace and the God of power—the tremendous power that raised Jesus from the dead. He's loving *and* He's able. His qualities don't stop there, though. He's peaceful, powerful, and personal. As the great shepherd of the sheep, He looks after His people—all of them. And finally, not only is He involved with His people, but He's also personally involved with me. He equips me. He works in me to do His will. That's the motivation found in our verses today. This God of peace, powerful enough to raise the dead, is the protector of His sheep, and He's seeing to it that I am prepared and able to accomplish His will. Threats and bribes and competition do nothing to make me do the will of God. Only God working in me will motivate me. Knowing that He is able and that He loves me enough to accomplish His will produces a faith that endures.

Read Today's Scripture:
Hebrews 13:17-25 and Philippians 2:13-16

1. How are we encouraged to act in Philippians 2:13-16? What motivates us to act this way?

2. What are some motivations in your life that have not lasted?

Today's Journal:

Please take a few minutes to reflect on all that you've learned in the book of Hebrews over the last eight weeks. Do you have a testimony you can share about your experience in God's Word? Can you share at least one example of how you are developing a faith that endures?

Final Thoughts

A recent *Washington Post* headline stated, "An America That Is Losing Faith with Religion." According to the Pew Foundation, the group of Americans with no religious affiliation was only 2 percent of the population in the 1950s, but it has grown to nearly 20 percent as of 2012.[29] Atheists claim that faith is believing in something you know is not true.[30] However, Christians believe in Someone who is true, powerful, and active.

Faith that endures. We began this journey by considering the object of our faith, Jesus, who is far superior to any other authority. At His invitation, we cease from our own works and enter His rest. Our invitation to enter the throne room of heaven is available only because Jesus died and rose again, and for no other reason. By faith we accept the payment on our behalf, and by faith we place our trust in His sacrifice. Without faith, it is impossible to please God.

Faith is credited as righteousness, as in the case of Abraham and the others in the "great cloud of witnesses" (Hebrews 12:1-2). Faith gives us a glimpse of our true citizenship and our true inheritance as children of God. Finally, God equips us to perform every work He has planned for us as He develops in us a faith that endures.

We have so many opportunities to place our faith somewhere other than in Jesus. We're tempted to place our faith in our jobs, our wealth, our physical ability, our families, or our friends. Even atheism requires faith—faith in our own superior intellect.

Only Jesus is reliable. He is superior, His work is superior, and He leads us to live superior lives. As we end this study, "Let us fix our eyes on Jesus, the author and perfecter of our faith" (Hebrews 12:2 NIV).

> In Christ alone my hope is found...
> Here in the love of Christ I stand.[31]

Endnotes

1. Grossman, C., 28 Dec 2007, "Young Adults Aren't Sticking with Church," *USA Today*, available online at http://usatoday30.usatoday.com/printedition/life/20070807/d_churchdropout07.art.htm

2. U.S. Religious Landscape Survey, 2007, Pew Forum on Religion & Public Life, available online at http://religions.pewforum.org/reports

3. Chambers, Oswald, 1992, *My Utmost for His Highest*. Updated edition, ed. James G. Reimann, Oswald Chambers Publications Association. Original edition © 1935 by Dodd, Mead & Company, Inc. December 3 devotion.

4. "In Christ Alone." Words and Music by Keith Getty & Stuart Townend. Copyright © 2002 Kingsway Thankyou Music.

5. Lennox, John. 2009. "Is Faith Delusional." Presentation at the ASU Open Forum. December 9, 2009.

6. Strong, James. 2001. *The New Strong's Expanded Exhaustive Concordance of the Bible,* Greek Dictionary of the New Testament, definition 4921, p. 242.

7. "Are the Days of Genesis To Be Interpreted Literally?" by Ted Cabal, *The Apologetics Study Bible,* 2007, Holman Bible Publishers, Nashville, TN. p.4.

8. Blackaby, Henry, Richard Blackaby, Thomas Blackaby, Melvin Blackaby, and Norman Blackaby. 2008. Hebrews Small Group Study, *Encounters With God*. Thomas Nelson Publishers, p. 15.

9   Chambers, Oswald, 1992, *My Utmost for His Highest*. Updated edition, ed. James G. Reimann, Oswald Chambers Publications Association. Original edition © 1935 by Dodd, Mead & Company, Inc. December 3 devotion.

10 For more information, see "Dancing House, Prague" available online at http://www.galinsky.com/buildings/dancinghouse/index.htm

11 Niccol, Andrew, writer. Peter Weir, director. 1998. *The Truman Show*. Hollywood, CA: Paramount Pictures.

12 "What Are Sleep Deprivation and Deficiency?" National Institutes of Health. Department of Health and Human Services. Updated 12 Feb 2012. Available online at http://www.nhlbi.nih.gov/health/health-topics/topics/sdd/

13 Hofstede, G. (2001). *Culture's Consequences: Comparing Values, Behaviors, Institutions, and Organizations Across Nations* (2nd Edition ed.). Thousand Oaks, CA: Sage Publications Inc.

14 Lea, Thomas. 1999. "Hebrews & James," *Holman New Testament Commentary*. ed. Max Anders, Broadman & Holman Publishers, Nashville, TN. p. 135.

15 Chafer, Lewis Sperry, 1917, *Salvation*, The Bible Institute Colportage Association.

16 Strong, James. 2001. *The New Strong's Expanded Exhaustive Concordance of the Bible*, Greek Dictionary of the New Testament, definition 4639, p. 228.

17 Strong, James. 2001. *The New Strong's Expanded Exhaustive Concordance of the Bible*, Greek Dictionary of the New Testament, definition 4983, p. 245.

18 See http://www.abagnale.com/index2.asp for more information.

19 Chambers, Oswald. 1992. *My Utmost for His Highest*. Updated edition, ed. James G. Reimann, Oswald Chambers Publications Association. Original edition © 1935 by Dodd, Mead & Company, Inc. December 8 devotion.

20 Alexander, Anila. May 3, 2012. "Kidnapped boy Nayati Moodliar found alive in Malaysia, Ransom paid by family for safe return," *International Business Times*, accessed online at http://www.ibtimes.com/kidnapped-boy-nayati-moodliar-found-alive-malaysia-ransom-paid-family-safe-return-695729#

21 Strong, James. 2001. *The New Strong's Expanded Exhaustive Concordance of the

Bible, Greek Dictionary of the New Testament, definition 5048, p. 248.

22   Strong, James. 2001. *The New Strong's Expanded Exhaustive Concordance of the Bible,* Greek Dictionary of the New Testament, definition 37, p. 3.

23   Carattini, Jill. "Great and Unsearchable" posted online July 3, 2012 available at http://www.rzim.org/a-slice-of-infinity/great-and-unsearchable/ original source C.S. Lewis, *God in the Dock.*

24   *Practical Word Studies in the New Testament,* 1998, Alpha-Omega Ministries, Inc. Leadership Ministries Worldwide, Chattanooga TN., p. 1205.

25   "The Psalmist Expresses His Affection for the Ordinances of God," Psalm 84, *Matthew Henry's Concise Commentary on the Bible,* available on the public domain and can be accessed at http://www.biblegateway.com/resources/commentaries/Matthew-Henry/Ps/Psalmist-Expresses-Affection

26   "My Faith Has Found a Resting Place," by Eliza E. Hewitt pub. 1891.

27   McVey, Steve, "Knowing the Will of God," Grace Walk Ministries, available online at <files.stablerack.com/WebFiles/69180/WillofGod.pdf> accessed 24 March 2013.

28   McVey, Steve, "Knowing the Will of God," Grace Walk Ministries, available online at <files.stablerack.com/WebFiles/69180/WillofGod.pdf> accessed 24 March 2013.

29   Gerson, Michael, "An America That Is Losing Faith with Religion," 26 March 2013, *Washington Post,* accessed online on 26 March 2013 at http://www.washingtonpost.com/opinions/michael-gerson-an-america-that-is-losing-faith-with-religion/2013/03/25/10d9fcb8-9582-11e2-bc8a-934ce979aa74_story.html?wpisrc=nl_headlines

30   Geisler, Norman and Frank Turek, 2004, *I Don't Have Enough Faith To Be an Atheist,* Crossway Books, Nashville.

31   "In Christ Alone." Words and Music by Keith Getty & Stuart Townend. Copyright © 2002 Kingsway Thankyou Music.

Acknowledgments

God has blessed me with a husband who practices Ephesians 5:25 and leads our family with kindness, gentleness, and wisdom. Thank you to my parents, Onsy and Susan Farag, for their encouragement and support, and for their courage to immigrate to a new world with a toddler so many years ago. To my children, Yasmeen and Joey, what a blessing you are to me. Thank you for the many stories that help me illustrate God's Word.

To Pastor E. Truman Herring of Boca Glades Baptist Church in Boca Raton, Florida—a mentor and friend to our family. I'm grateful to have sat under your teaching all these years. To our dear friends, Pastor Paul Waters and Mary Jane Waters, thank you for your encouragement and love. To the ladies at Myrtle Grove Baptist Church who have tirelessly studied the Bible with me and who allowed me the privilege of teaching this book several years ago. Thank you.

Thank you to my friends and family who read through the final manuscript in search of any last edits. Yasmeen, you have a future as a copy editor. For your help with the book launch, thank you Meaghan Burnett. To my editor, Denise Loock, and publisher, Eddie Jones of Lighthouse Publishing of the Carolinas, thank you for your willingness to work with me.

Made in the USA
Middletown, DE
04 August 2021